10647577

THE PHOTO GRAPHY SHOW

PRESENTED BY AIPAD

THE PH●TO GRAPHY SHOW

PRESENTED BY AIPAD

2019 Membership Directory and Illustrated Catalogue

ADDRESS	2025 M Street NW, Suite 800
	Washington, DC 20036 USA
PHONE	+1-202-367-1158
FAX	+1-202-367-2158
EMAIL	info@aipad.com
WEB	AIPAD.com

The Association of International
Photography Art Dealers

*Premier Corporate
Partner of AIPAD*

*Official Printing
Partner of AIPAD*

EASTWOOD LITHO

2019 Membership Directory and Illustrated Catalogue

©2019 AIPAD Membership Directory and Illustrated Catalogue
ISBN: 1-893590-09-7
ISSN: 1554-138X

Table of Contents

 The Association of International
Photography Art Dealers

About the Association of International Photography Art Dealers

The Association of International Photography Art Dealers (AIPAD) was organized in 1979. With members in the United States, Australia, Canada, Europe, and Japan, the Association has become a unifying force in the field of photography. AIPAD is dedicated to creating and maintaining high standards in the business of exhibiting, buying, and selling photographs as art.

Acting as the collective voice of the art photography dealers that make up its membership, AIPAD maintains ethical standards, promotes communication within the photographic community, encourages public appreciation of photography as art, concerns itself with the rights of photographers and collectors, and works to enhance the confidence of the public in responsible photography. AIPAD members provide a wide range of services to the public, such as exhibitions, appraisals, expert opinions, and consultations.

AIPAD members have agreed to a Code of Ethics: members agree to conduct dealings with the public, museums, artists, and other dealers with honesty and integrity. Members agree to provide accurate descriptions of photographs in all disclosures, including but not limited to, invoices, wall labels, and price lists. AIPAD members must meet a number of criteria for at least five years prior to joining the Association, including: 1) a significant portion of a member's business must be devoted to the sale and promotion of fine art photography which meet the Association's high artistic standards; 2) members must have a reputation in the community for honesty and integrity, both generally and in dealings with the public, museums, photographers, and other dealers; and 3) members must demonstrate that they are making substantial contributions to the field of fine art photography through the quality of photographic art offered for sale, exhibitions mounted, or catalogues published. New members are invited to join the Association by the Board of Directors.

For more information, visit AIPAD online at AIPAD.com.

I. AIPAD 2019 Board of Directors

AIPAD 2019 Board of Directors

PRESIDENT
Richard Moore
RICHARD MOORE PHOTOGRAPHS

PRESIDENT ELECT
Roland Baron
GALLERY 19/21

TREASURER
Karen Marks
HOWARD GREENBERG GALLERY

SECRETARY
Caroline Wall
ROBERT MANN GALLERY

IMMEDIATE PAST PRESIDENT
Terry Etherton
ETHERTON GALLERY

DIRECTORS
Julie Castellano
EDWYNN HOUK GALLERY

Stephen Daiter
STEPHEN DAITER GALLERY

Michael Lee
LEE GALLERY

Larry Miller
LAURENCE MILLER GALLERY

Andra Russek
SCHEINBAUM & RUSSEK LTD.

Lisa Sette
LISA SETTE GALLERY

Rick Wester
RICK WESTER FINE ART

II. Welcome Messages

President's Message

Welcome to the 39th edition of The Photography Show presented by AIPAD. We are pleased to return to Pier 94 for the third year as we continue to focus and refine the Show experience for all exhibitors and attendees.

As a nonprofit association comprised of fine art photography galleries and dealers, AIPAD continues to provide an unparalleled platform for viewing the best in the photographic medium, welcoming leading gallerists, book dealers, publishers, and photography-related organizations from around the world to this year's Show. New this year, project spaces will highlight a curated selection of solo artist and themed presentations. In addition, AIPAD will host a special exhibition, curated by artist Alec Soth, entitled *A Room for Solace: An Exhibition of Domestic Interiors*. Soth will draw from historical photography through the present day to address how photographers build a community by revealing the enduring spirit of humanity that unites us all.

Our third annual AIPAD Award will honor Sarah Greenough, Senior Curator and Head of the Department of Photographs at the National Gallery of Art, Washington, DC – a visionary who has contributed enormously to the field of photography. We will also honor the memory of AIPAD founding member and past president Tom Halsted, whose pioneering gallery celebrates its 50th year in 2019. The AIPAD Talks program will continue with dynamic presentations featuring eminent collectors, curators, critics, and gallerists.

Please join me in giving sincere thanks to AXA Art, our premier corporate partner, who has supported AIPAD for more than a decade. Together, AXA Art and AIPAD continue to uphold and promote the highest standards for exhibiting, buying, and selling photography and media-based arts.

Thank you for attending the longest-running and foremost exhibition dedicated to the photographic medium — we hope you enjoy the Show!

Best regards,

Richard Moore
AIPAD President

Welcome to The Photography Show

AXA Art Americas Corporation, the proud Premier Corporate Partner of the Association of International Photography Art Dealers, hopes you share our enthusiastic welcome for this 39th edition of The Photography Show presented by AIPAD, now in its third year at Pier 94.

This year also celebrates AXA Art Americas Corporation's 11-year partnership with AIPAD.

As fine art and collectibles specialist insurers, we value our longstanding work with AIPAD. This distinguished organization continues to set the highest standards in exhibiting, selling, and promoting photography as an exciting branch of fine art. Through gallery exhibitions, rich educational programming, catalogues, and acclaimed photography fairs, AIPAD's work has been central to the growth of photography's audience and the growing body of scholarship.

While the work of the AIPAD membership is all year-round, their most visible event certainly is The Photography Show held each spring in New York. The event showcases work from both AIPAD members and new exhibitors, as well as younger galleries, book dealers, and publishers. We are looking forward to experiencing the wide range of photography, but also photo-based art and video by artists from all over the world that these exhibitors will bring to New York.

Please join all of us at AXA Art in congratulating AIPAD on their past accomplishments and this year's new edition of The Photography Show!

We look forward with great anticipation to this year's lineup and hope to see you at the Show!

AXA Art Americas Corporation

April 4, 2019

Dear Friends:

It is a pleasure to welcome everyone to The Photography Show at Pier 94, hosted by the Association of International Photography Art Dealers.

As a global hub of creativity and the arts, New York is the perfect home for the world's longest-running exhibition dedicated to the photographic medium. Now in its 39th year, the Show features more than 100 leading fine art galleries, booksellers, and publishers presenting diverse works by emerging and established photographers of all backgrounds. Attracting artists, dealers, collectors and enthusiasts from the five boroughs and beyond, this terrific event provides attendees the chance to network, discover new talent, and learn more about trends and advancements in the disciplines of photography, video, and new media. I am delighted to applaud AIPAD's members and everyone associated with this inspiring showcase for all they do to captivate New Yorkers through the power of photography and enhance the cultural vibrancy of our great city.

On behalf of the City of New York, I offer my best wishes for a wonderful show and an enjoyable stay for all those visiting the five boroughs for this exciting event.

Sincerely,

Bill de Blasio
Mayor

III. Partners and Sponsors

Thank You to our Partners and Sponsors

Premier Corporate Partner of AIPAD

SIDLEY

Official Online Partner

EASTWOOD LITHO

Official Printing Partner

Official Shipping Partner

Additional Sponsors

Media Partners

IV. AIPAD Talks

AIPAD Talks

The Photography Show presented by AIPAD brings together prominent curators, artists, collectors, and writers to discuss thought-provoking ideas, new trends, and unique processes involved in the medium of photography. AIPAD Talks start conversations that lead to understanding, inspiration, and action.

Topics and speakers are subject to change

Thursday, April 4
12:30 p.m. – 1:30 p.m.
ARTIST TALK: DAWOUD BEY
With Corey Keller, Curator of Photography, San Francisco Museum of Modern Art
Dawoud Bey is an American photographer acclaimed for his powerful portraits of underrepresented or even unseen subjects and landscapes that meditate on African-American experience. The recipient of numerous awards, Bey was honored in 2018 with a MacArthur Foundation Fellowship. A major survey exhibition of his work, *Dawoud Bey: An American Project*, is being co-organized by the San Francisco Museum of Modern Art and the Whitney Museum of American Art, opening in 2020.

2:00 p.m. – 3:00 p.m.
THE QUEER TRAJECTORY: PHOTOGRAPHY SINCE STONEWALL
Chris Boot, Executive Director, Aperture, with Sophie Hackett, Curator of Photography, Art Gallery of Ontario; Matthew Leifheit, Artist and Editor of MATTE Magazine; and Antwaun Sargent, Writer and Critic
Photography and the evolution of LGBTQ art and identities, fifty years since Stonewall. Three curatorial and editorial influencers, who are contributing to Aperture publishing programs, will present photographic works they are engaged with that speak to this story, followed by a discussion.

3:30 p.m. – 4:30 p.m.

CURATOR TALK: SARAH GREENOUGH

Senior Curator, Head of the Department of Photographs, National Gallery of Art, Washington, DC
Building a personal collection of photographs can be a thrilling experience. But when Sarah Greenough was given the project of forming a collection for the National Gallery of Art, the mission took on greater proportions. See what made the cut and why.

5:00 p.m. – 6:00 p.m.

THESE PEOPLE, THIS PLACE: ART AND REPRESENTATION

Sarah Hermanson Meister, Curator, The Museum of Modern Art, with Artists Deana Lawson, An-My Lê, and Rosalind Solomon
Sarah Hermanson Meister invites three leading artists, whose work engages with questions of representation, voice, and the role of the photographic document, to join her in a conversation, inspired in part by her current projects at MoMA (a book about Frances Benjamin Johnston's Hampton Album and *Dorothea Lange: Words and Pictures*, a forthcoming exhibition and catalogue).

AIPAD Talks require separate admission

Friday, April 5

12:30 p.m. – 1:30 p.m.

BETWEEN THE LINES: SURVEYING THE ORIGINAL U.S.-MEXICO BORDER
Dr. Rebecca Senf, Chief Curator, Center for Creative Photography, University of Arizona, with Artists Marcos Ramírez ERRE and David Taylor

Two artists, one Mexican and one American, set out to reframe the history of the U.S.-Mexico border with a 2,400-mile-long site specific installation *DeLIMITations*. Telling their story through photography, video, and maps, the artists discuss their 2014 collaboration to trace the boundary as it existed in 1821, when it encompassed all of present day California, Nevada, Utah, Arizona, New Mexico, and Texas as well as portions of four other states.

2:00 p.m. – 3:00 p.m.

CONTEMPORARY IDEAS IN PHOTOGRAPHY'S PAST
Malcolm Daniel, Gus and Lyndall Wortham Curator of Photography, The Museum of Fine Arts, Houston

A specialist in the early history of the medium, Malcolm Daniel hopes to entice collectors and enthusiasts to a greater exploration and appreciation of 19th-century photography by making connections between the past and the present. Ideas and approaches that are familiar and exciting in contemporary photography – image manipulation, staged photography, materiality and process, acceptance of chance, performance – provide pathways to less familiar aspects of the medium's rich history.

AIPAD Talks require separate admission

3:30 p.m. – 4:30 p.m.
ARTIST TALK: MARTHA WILSON
With Jarrett Earnest, Writer and Art Critic
Over the past four decades, the pioneering feminist artist Martha Wilson has created innovative photographic and video work that explores her female subjectivity though transformational self-portraits and "invasions" of other people's personae. For this AIPAD Talk, she offers a rare opportunity to see her new work in the context of her signature work.

5:00 p.m. – 6:00 p.m.
ARTIST TALK: STEPHEN SHORE
With Lynne Tillman, Novelist, Essayist, and Art Critic
World-renowned photographer Stephen Shore, in conversation with writer Lynne Tillman, discusses the intricacies and nuances of the artistic process. How do artists and writers use raw experiences to build pictures and stories? Is there pressure to communicate in ways less mediated by convention and genre?

AIPAD Talks require separate admission

Saturday, April 6

12:30 p.m. – 1:30 p.m.

ARTIST TALK: HARRY BENSON

Harry Benson arrived on the plane with the Beatles in 1964 and never looked back. He has photographed every president from Eisenhower to Trump; marched with Dr. Martin Luther King Jr. during the Civil Rights movement; was next to Senator Bobby Kennedy when he was assassinated; and recently photographed Queen Elizabeth II for her official portrait for the National Portrait Gallery of Scotland. The recipient of three honorary doctorates and the International Center of Photography's Lifetime Achievement Award, Benson was made a Commander of the Order of the British Empire for service to photography. No other photographer has the track record of the one and only Harry Benson.

2:00 p.m. – 3:00 p.m.

YOU WERE THERE: ARCHIVAL PHOTOGRAPHY THAT BRINGS FILMS TO LIFE

Erik Taros, Filmmaker, Archive Specialist (Ron Howard's Eight Days a Week), and Multimedia Artist; Amei Wallach, Author, Critic, and Filmmaker (Taking Venice: The Rauschenberg Factor); Kathy Brew, Guest Curator, Doc Fortnight, The Museum of Modern Art and Independent Filmmaker (Moderator)

How do documentary films evoke and establish a sense of time and place? Leading filmmakers discuss the role of archival photographs in films about the Beatles, Robert Rauschenberg, and other artists, and how they set the stage for narrative, nuance, and identity.

AIPAD Talks require separate admission

3:30 p.m. – 4:30 p.m.
PHOTOJOURNALISM IN THE MEDIA AGE
With James Estrin, and David Gonzales, Co-Editors, The New York Times Lens Blog
On the occasion of the 10th anniversary of *Lens*, the co-editors will review the last decade of photography and explore the future of the medium.

5:00 p.m. – 6:00 p.m.
AUTHOR TALK: VINCE ALETTI
With Carol Squiers, Writer, Curator
The former *Village Voice* and *New Yorker* critic previews his upcoming book, *Issues: A History of Photography in Fashion Magazines* (Phaidon, April 2019) on 100 of the most important fashion magazine issues from the 1920s to the present.

AIPAD Talks require separate admission

V. Special Exhibition, Project Spaces, and Other Projects

Special Exhibition Curated by Alec Soth

A Room for Solace: An Exhibition of Domestic Interiors

With this exhibition, Alec Soth wants to take a break from the fractious public square of photography and wander quietly into people's homes. Behind these doors, he hopes to find a sliver of solace in these unstable times. This special exhibition curated for The Photography Show will feature domestic interiors that speak to the possibility of finding refuge during turbulent times.

Alec Soth is a photographer born and based in Minneapolis, Minnesota. He has published over twenty-five books including *Sleeping by the Mississippi* (2004), *NIAGARA* (2006), *Broken Manual* (2010), and *Songbook* (2015). Soth has had over fifty solo exhibitions including survey shows organized by Jeu de Paume in Paris (2008), the Walker Art Center in Minnesota (2010) and Media Space in London (2015). Soth has been the recipient of numerous fellowships and awards, including the Guggenheim Fellowship (2013). In 2008, Soth created Little Brown Mushroom, a multi-media enterprise focused on visual storytelling. Soth is represented by Sean Kelly in New York, Weinstein Hammons Gallery in Minneapolis, Fraenkel Gallery in San Francisco, Loock Gallery in Berlin and is a member of Magnum Photos.

Alec Soth

Project Spaces

New in 2019, project spaces showcase a single artist presentation or are curated around a specific project, theme, or idea.

An asterisk(*) denotes galleries exhibiting at The Photography Show, presented by AIPAD

American Society of Media Photographers, New York, NY

Blanca Berlin Gallery, Madrid, Spain

Catherine Couturier Gallery, Houston, TX*

ClampArt, New York, NY*

Contemporary Works/Vintage Works, Chalfont, PA*

Duncan Miller Gallery, Malibu, CA

Etherton Gallery, Tucson, AZ*, and **Stephen Daiter Gallery,** Chicago, IL*

galerie SIT DOWN, Paris, France

KAMOINGE, INC., New York, NY

Keith de Lellis Gallery, New York, NY*

Kopeikin Gallery, Los Angeles, CA

Momentum Fine Art, Miami, FL*

Morehouse Gallery, Laredo, TX

Peter Fetterman Gallery, Santa Monica, CA*

photo-eye, Santa Fe, NM*

Rick Wester Fine Art, New York, NY

Robert Mann Gallery, New York, NY*

SoPhoto Gallery, Beijing, China

Staley-Wise Gallery, New York, NY*

Stephen Bulger Gallery, Toronto, Canada, and **Pierre-François Oullette art contemporain,** Montreal, Canada

Taylor Graham, New York, NY

VRG, Ap Lei Chau, Hong Kong

Yancey Richardson Gallery, New York, NY*

Other Projects

The PhotoBook Spotlight, presented by *Aperture*

The PhotoBook Spotlight, presented by *Aperture*, celebrates the contribution of the photobook to the evolving story of photography. *Aperture* will present a daily, in-person spotlight on individual books and publishers. Visit AIPADShow.com for the schedule and featured guests.

Exhibitor-Hosted Events

Exhibitors will host events in their booths and exhibit spaces during the Show including artist book signings and meet and greets. These events are free with a valid Show admission ticket and open to the public. Visit AIPADShow.com to view the schedule.

VI. The AIPAD Award

The AIPAD Award

The AIPAD Award was established to honor and recognize visionaries who have spent their lives at the forefront of the field of photography. The 2019 AIPAD Award will be presented during the Opening Preview on April 3.

Sarah Greenough

Sarah Greenough is senior curator and head of the department of photographs at the National Gallery of Art, Washington, DC. Prior to coming to the Gallery, Greenough received her B.A. at the University of Pennsylvania and her M.A. and Ph.D. at the University of New Mexico where she studied with the noted photographic historian Beaumont Newhall. In 1978, she was awarded a Samuel H. Kress Fellowship at the Gallery, where she has worked ever since. In 1990, she became the founding curator of the department of photographs and has been responsible for establishing and growing the National Gallery's collection of photographs, which now numbers more than 17,000 works made between 1839 and the present. She also established the program for photography at the National Gallery, which now presents two to three photography exhibitions per year in the museum's dedicated photography galleries, as well as many smaller installations.

Greenough is the recipient of many awards and is the author of many publications, including *Walker Evans: Subways and Streets* (1991), *Robert Frank: Moving Out* (1994), *Harry Callahan* (1996), *Alfred Stieglitz: The Key Set* (2002), *All the Mighty World: The Photographs of Roger Fenton,* 1852–1860 (2004), with Malcolm Daniel and Gordon Baldwin, *The Altering Eye: Photographs from the National Gallery of Art* (2015), with Sarah Kennel, Andrea Nelson, Diane Waggoner, and Philip Brookman, and author and editor of *My Faraway One: Selected Letters of Georgia O'Keeffe and Alfred Stieglitz, Volume One,* 1915-1933, Yale University Press (2011).

VII. In Memoriam

In Memoriam

Tom Halsted
1937-2018

Tom Halsted was born on July 12, 1937, in Birmingham, Michigan. He graduated from Birmingham High School and attended Ferris State University as well as Miami University. He was always interested in photography, working at the local camera store in high school as well as being the photographer for the school paper. He was a drummer in a band with his lifelong friends, one of whom was Paul Stookey of Peter Paul and Mary, whom he joined in New York in 1960. He took photographs for groups like Bob Dillon and Joan Bias. It was then he began taking pictures seriously.

Meeting his wife, Carol in New York in 1963, he married, and they both returned to their hometown of Birmingham, Michigan. They had two children, Wendy and Andy, and settled into a quieter life. He began an advertising photography business while taking fine art images on the side. In 1969, he had the idea of starting a fine art photography gallery where he could sell images by artists he admired such as Adams, Weston, Stieglitz, and many more. The gallery's first exhibit was a show of Eugène Atget, images that Tom acquired from his friend and photographer Berenice Abbott. Early exhibitions were a mix of accomplished photographers and young unknowns. At the time, there were around six galleries in the country dedicated to fine art photography. Today, the industry has grown to hundreds of galleries.

At that time, he spent most of his efforts educating people about fine art photography and fighting for its place in the art world. He forged friendships with some of the great photographers, such as Ansel Adams, André Kertész, Berenice Abbott, Harry Callahan, Imogen Cunningham, and many, many more. He helped build collectable markets for their images and those of many others. He worked with these photographers on the business of art in establishing prices, marketing, and other "nuts and bolts" of the business. He taught people how to look at a photograph and why they were special and deserving of the designation of art. He sold to museums and collectors all over the country. He had many of the great photographers at the gallery. Ansel Adams came the first time in 1972 to a crowd of 50 people. At Adams' last visit in 1984, there were over 500 people lined up around the block to get into the gallery. Tom represented many estates over the years, enjoying most representing August Sander Estate and working with his son, Gunther, in Germany. There was always an opening for a new exhibit at the gallery and the photographers made an effort to attend. Tom was also a founding member of AIPAD as well as the second president of the organization.

Tom Halsted lived to see his legacy reach 50 years. The gallery celebrates its 50th birthday this year, making it the oldest in the country dedicated to fine art photography. The gallery is currently run by his daughter, Wendy.

Tom loved his family, photography, and Michigan football. He would often say a photograph should make your life better every day. It was Tom who made life better for those around him every day.

Charles Schwartz
1938-2019

I first met Charles in 1979, when he signed up for one of my Collector's Seminars, which I taught to try to encourage new collectors through education. The seminars answered the question of what makes for value in photography. Charles was more interested in that question than in art history. He was a buyer and a businessman, and he wanted to acquire work using criteria other than pure instinct. He wasn't a novice exactly, as he had been collecting daguerreotypes and other mostly "cased" imagery as far back as college. In fact, Charles was a founding member of the Daguerreian Society. He also opened one of the first galleries in the then new SoHo art district...before anyone had even heard of Chelsea.

His day job was running Elmhurst Dairy, a family-owned business he inherited from his father. It was a large operation that supplied New York with about 25 percent of its milk. It was a highly competitive business, with a lot of moving parts that brought milk from the cows spread all around the New York area to your grocer's refrigerator cases and all the way to your morning coffee. He was steady and shrewd, fielding an ocean of details, and that's how he treated collecting – understanding the details without losing touch with the fun.

Charles used his milk money to support his photography collecting but felt his time being taken by two demanding masters. So, in 1987, Charles sold the dairy and concentrated on photography, his first love. He did the buying circuit as we all did... the auctions here and abroad, trade shows, and early morning raids at Brimfield carried out by flashlight in the dark at 6 a.m. Charles had developed his own areas of interest: a nostalgic group of dairy-related imagery; photographers photographing; people reading; and early images of New York, for example, Victor Prevost's pictures of the building of Central Park. These were exemplary but somewhat prosaic. His more exciting addictions were often the result of good old-fashioned digging in unfurrowed fields. One of my favorite patented Schwartz collections is what Charles called his "Double Vintage" collection, wherein vintage images would share a frame with the very object being pictured. One of the most eerie was a daguerreotype of a very young girl in a gingham dress. The dress was included in the frame, next to the daguerreotype of it. Then there was his Japanese Ambrotype collection whose delicate images on glass were contained in beautiful handcrafted Kiriwood cases.

Charles' devotion to early photography led him to build a huge room-size Camera Obscura on the roof of his elegant triplex penthouse overlooking the Cooper-Hewitt museum gardens and Central Park beyond. The Camera Obscura, of course, was where photography began. Its name comes from the Latin for "dark room," which is exactly what it was and what Charles built. Instead of the usual small aperture in one of the walls, which allowed for light reflecting off an object outside of the room to be projected upside down on the opposite wall, he used the later improvement of a lens. The custom fabricated lens was able to gather and focus the light for a cleaner and sharper effect. The specially designed lens was a periscope-like device which protruded through the roof and threw its image onto a perfectly flat 42" round table, which Charles then photographed. Charles' Camera Obscura work, produced in partnership with Bill Westheimer, used the oldest image gathering device to produce contemporary work bearing little similarity to the device's original spawn. That is to say, they did not look like rehashed new old things, they were completely of today with perhaps only a nod given to their predecessors.

Around the same time as the construction of his Camera Obscura, Charles was contacted by Shawn Wilson, a filmmaker from Greenville, Mississippi, about an entire archive of a local photographer, Henry Clay Anderson. He was the general practitioner photographer of Greenville's African-American community. For decades, he documented their daily lives, their families, their relationship with their church, and to each other. Rather than showing the oppressive aspects of life under legal segregation, he showed their middle class aspirations, their progress, their joys and sorrows. In short, lives of normalcy and connection. Charles and Shawn conserved the prints and negatives and produced a critically acclaimed book on Anderson's work, *Separate but Equal*. The entire Anderson archive now resides at the National Museum of African American History and Culture in Washington, DC., thus saving them from oblivion.

The final collection to note was what he called his "Light Reclaimed" collection. Charles explains, "For over 35 years I have collected daguerreotypes, ambrotypes and tintypes. In collecting these images, I usually looked for a perfect, flawless piece, but over time, especially at flea markets, I found myself drawn to boxes containing the undesirable – broken, scratched, partially destroyed images where the imperfections, rather than ruining the object, seemed to impart a greater beauty. I kept these flawed treasures in a box and called them 'my orphans.' Eventually he started to scan his "orphans," emphasizing their new scale and their new stress derived meaning, without altering time's hand on the object. They are really artist-less art... fortunately, in Charles, they found a curator!

Charles was a hard man to pin down. He was a dealer with a very refined taste, a curator of collections both for his clients, and those amassed solely for himself. Once he got hooked by something, he made sure a good deal of research was done to back it up historically, and critically. This was made more difficult by the fact that Charles was dyslexic and was forced to routinely employ an elaborate system of workarounds to keep things on-track. Fortunately, with Jennie Hirschfeld, he had an amanuensis who was a great researcher and writer. They were devoted to each other. Charles' label descriptions always made for interesting reading. Finally, there were his artistic endeavors. Could you have a fabulously functioning high-tech Camera Obscura and not use it? Certainly not, and not only did he make lyrical and imaginative pictures with it, but he lived in it. His desk, his flat files, his fireproof safe, the etched glass doors to the room showing Nadar in the gondola of a hot air balloon (no accident that), were all inside the Camera itself. This was only appropriate, as Charles was certainly a total immersion kind of guy.

– Alan Klotz, Alan Klotz Gallery, AIPAD Member, and Friend

In Memoriam

Gloria Katz Huyck
1942-2018

Collector and champion of photography, Gloria Katz Huyck passed away on November 25, 2018. She and her husband, Willard, were passionate collectors of Japanese photography and placed their collection with the Freer/Sackler Galleries in Washington, DC earlier this year. In addition to collaborating with Manfred Heiting and Steidel on *Views of Japan from the Gloria Katz & Willard Huyck Collection*, Gloria served as the former chair of LACMA's Photo Council, co-founder and chair of the Photographic Arts Council of Los Angeles, and member of the Getty Museum Photographs Council.

VIII. 2019 Membership Directory

2019 Membership Directory

Alan Klotz Gallery*

ADDRESS 740 West End Avenue
Suite 52
New York, NY 10025
PHONE 212-741-4764
EMAIL info@klotzgallery.com
WEB klotzgallery.com

Alexander / Vasari

ADDRESS New York, Buenos Aires
41 East 57th Street, Suite 704
New York, NY 10022
PHONE 212-315-2211
EMAIL info@nailyaalexandergallery.com
WEB nailyaalexandergallery.com

Arnika Dawkins Gallery Photographic Fine Art*

ADDRESS 4600 Cascade Road
Atlanta, GA 30331
PHONE 404-333-0312
EMAIL agd@adawkinsgallery.com
WEB arnikadawkins.com

Atlas Gallery*

ADDRESS 49 Dorset Street
London, United Kingdom
W1U 7NF
PHONE +44 (0)20 7224 4192
EMAIL info@atlasgallery.com
WEB atlasgallery.com

Augusta Edwards Fine Art*

ADDRESS 61 Willow Walk
First Floor
London, United Kingdom
SE1 5SF
PHONE +44 20 7064 1070
EMAIL info@augustaedwards.com
WEB augustaedwards.com

Barry Singer Gallery*

ADDRESS PO Box 2658
Petaluma, CA 94953
PHONE 707-781-3200
EMAIL gretchen@singergallery.com
WEB singergallery.com

baudoin lebon*

ADDRESS 8 rue Charles-François Dupuis
Paris, France 75003
PHONE +33 1 42 72 09 10
EMAIL info@baudoin-lebon.com
WEB baudoin-lebon.com

Bruce Silverstein Gallery*

ADDRESS 529 West 20th Street
3rd Floor
New York, NY 10011
PHONE 212-627-3930
EMAIL inquiries@brucesilverstein.com
WEB brucesilverstein.com

Bryce Wolkowitz Gallery*

ADDRESS 505 West 24th Street
New York, NY 10011
PHONE 212-243-8830
EMAIL info@brycewolkowitz.com
WEB brycewolkowitz.com

Catherine Couturier Gallery*

ADDRESS 2635 Colquitt Street
Houston, TX 77098
PHONE 713-524-5070
EMAIL gallery@catherinecouturier.com
WEB catherinecouturier.com

An asterisk(*) denotes galleries exhibiting at The Photography Show presented by AIPAD

Catherine Edelman Gallery*

ADDRESS	1637 West Chicago Avenue
	Chicago, IL 60622
PHONE	312-266-2350
EMAIL	info@edelmangallery.com
WEB	edelmangallery.com

Charles A. Hartman Fine Art

ADDRESS	134 Northwest 8th Avenue
	Portland, OR 97209
PHONE	503-287-3886
EMAIL	charles@hartmanfineart.net
WEB	hartmanfineart.net

Charles Isaacs Photographs, Inc.*

ADDRESS	25 West 54th Street
	Suite 5CD
	New York, NY 10019
PHONE	212-957-3238
EMAIL	cti@charlesisaacs.com
WEB	charlesisaacs.com

ClampArt*

ADDRESS	247 West 29th Street
	Ground Floor
	New York, NY 10001
PHONE	646-230-0020
EMAIL	info@clampart.com
WEB	clampart.com

Contemporary Works/Vintage Works*

ADDRESS	258 Inverness Circle
	Chalfont, PA 18914
PHONE	215-822-5662
EMAIL	info@vintageworks.net
WEB	vintageworks.net

Daniel Blau

ADDRESS	Maximilianstrasse 26
	Munich, Germany 80539
PHONE	+49 (89) 29 73 42
EMAIL	contact@danielblau.com
WEB	danielblau.com

Danziger Gallery

ADDRESS	980 Madison Avenue
	Third Floor
	New York, NY 10075
PHONE	212-629-6778
EMAIL	info@danzigergallery.com
WEB	danzigergallery.com

DC Moore Gallery

ADDRESS	535 West 22nd Street
	2nd Floor
	New York, NY 10011
PHONE	212-247-2111
EMAIL	info@dcmooregallery.com
WEB	dcmooregallery.com

Deborah Bell Photographs*

ADDRESS	16 East 71st Street
	Suite 1D, 4th Floor
	New York, NY 10021
PHONE	212-249-9400
EMAIL	info@deborahbellphotographs.com
WEB	deborahbellphotographs.com

Edwynn Houk Gallery*

ADDRESS	745 Fifth Avenue
	New York, NY 10151
PHONE	212-750-7070
EMAIL	info@houkgallery.com
WEB	houkgallery.com

2019 Membership Directory

Etherton Gallery*

ADDRESS 135 South 6th Avenue
Tucson, AZ 85701
PHONE 520-624-7370
EMAIL info@ethertongallery.com
WEB ethertongallery.com

Ezra Mack

ADDRESS 645 G Street
Suite 100-589
Anchorage, AK 99501
PHONE 310-752-3454
EMAIL fineartcom@aol.com

Fahey/Klein Gallery*

ADDRESS 148 North La Brea Avenue
Los Angeles, CA 90036
PHONE 323-934-2250
EMAIL contact@faheykleingallery.com
WEB faheykleingallery.com

Flowers Gallery*

ADDRESS 529 West 20th Street
New York, NY 10011
PHONE 212-439-1700
EMAIL newyork@flowersgallery.com
WEB flowersgallery.com

Fraenkel Gallery

ADDRESS 49 Geary Street
4th Floor
San Francisco, CA 94108
PHONE 415-981-2661
EMAIL mail@fraenkelgallery.com
WEB fraenkelgallery.com

G. Gibson Gallery

ADDRESS 104 West Roy Street
Seattle, WA 98119
PHONE 206-587-4033
EMAIL gail@ggibsongallery.com
WEB ggibsongallery.com

Galerie f5,6*

ADDRESS Lydwigstraße 7
München, Bayern, Germany
PHONE +49 89 28675167
EMAIL info@f56.net
WEB f56.net

Galerie Johannes Faber

ADDRESS Brahmsplatz 7
Vienna, Austria 01040
PHONE +43 1 505 75 18
EMAIL office@jmcfaber.at
WEB jmcfaber.at

Galerie Karsten Greve

ADDRESS Drususgasse 1-5
Cologne, Germany 50667
PHONE +49 (0)221 257 10 12
EMAIL info@galerie-karsten-greve.de
WEB galerie-karsten-greve.com

Gallery 19/21*

ADDRESS 9 Little Harbor Road
Guilford, CT 06437
PHONE 857-991-1822
EMAIL gallery19th21st@aol.com
WEB gallery19-21.com

GALLERY FIFTY ONE

ADDRESS   Zirkstraat 20
Antwerp, Belgium 02000
PHONE   +32 (0)3 289 84 58
EMAIL   info@gallery51.com
WEB   gallery51.com

Gary Edwards Gallery*

ADDRESS   14 Wolf Swamp Lane
Southampton, NY 11968
PHONE   301-524-0900
EMAIL   garymedwards@mac.com

Gilles Peyroulet & Cie*

ADDRESS   75+80 rue Quincampoix
Paris, France 75003
PHONE   +33 (0)1 42 78 85 11
EMAIL   contact@galeriepeyroulet.com
WEB   galeriepeyroulet.com

Gitterman Gallery*

ADDRESS   41 East 57th Street
Suite 1103
New York, NY 10022
PHONE   212-734-0868
EMAIL   info@gittermangallery.com
WEB   gittermangallery.com

HackelBury Fine Art*

ADDRESS   4 Launceston Place
London, United Kingdom
W8 5RL
PHONE   +44 20 7937 8688
EMAIL   gallery@hackelbury.co.uk
WEB   hackelbury.co.uk

The Halsted Gallery*

ADDRESS   2234 Cole Street
Birmingham, MI 48009
PHONE   248-895-0204
EMAIL   wendy@halstedgallery.com
WEB   halstedgallery.com

Hans P. Kraus Jr. Inc.*

ADDRESS   962 Park Avenue
New York, NY 10028
PHONE   212-794-2064
EMAIL   info@sunpictures.com
WEB   sunpictures.com

Henry Feldstein

ADDRESS   PO Box 398
Forest Hills, NY 11375
PHONE   718-544-3002
EMAIL   henryfe@ix.netcom.com

Holden Luntz Gallery, Inc.*

ADDRESS   332 Worth Avenue
Palm Beach, FL 33480
PHONE   561-805-9550
EMAIL   info@holdenluntz.com
WEB   holdenluntz.com

Howard Greenberg Gallery*

ADDRESS   41 East 57th Street
Suite 1406
New York, NY 10022
PHONE   212-334-0010
EMAIL   info@howardgreenberg.com
WEB   howardgreenberg.com

2019 Membership Directory

Huxley-Parlour Gallery*

ADDRESS 3-5 Swallow Street
London, United Kingdom
W1B 4DE
PHONE +44 020 7434 4319
EMAIL gallery@huxleyparlour.com
WEB huxleyparlour.com

Hyperion Press, Ltd.

ADDRESS 200 West 86th Street
New York, NY 10024
PHONE 212-877-2131
EMAIL hyperionpr@verizon.net
WEB hyperionpressltd.com

IBASHO*

ADDRESS Tolstraat 67
2000 Antwerp, Belgium
PHONE +32 (0)32162028
EMAIL info@ibashogallery.com
WEB ibashogallery.com

Jackson Fine Art*

ADDRESS 3115 East Shadowlawn Avenue
Northeast
Atlanta, GA 30305
PHONE 404-233-3739
EMAIL courney@jacksonfineart.com
WEB jacksonfineart.com

James Hyman Gallery*

ADDRESS PO Box 67698
London, United Kingdom
NW11 1NE
PHONE +44 (0)207 494 3857
EMAIL info@jameshymangallery.com
WEB jameshymangallery.com

Jenkins Johnson Gallery

ADDRESS 464 Sutter Street
San Francisco, CA 94108
PHONE 415-677-0770
EMAIL sf@jenkinsjohnsongallery.com
WEB jenkinsjohnsongallery.com

Joel Soroka Gallery*

ADDRESS PO Box 1226
Aspen, CO 81612
PHONE 970-923-4393
EMAIL joelsorokagallery@gmail.com
WEB joelsorokagallery.com

Jörg Maaß Kunsthandel*

ADDRESS Rankestraße 24
Berlin, Germany 10789
PHONE +49 (0)30 211 54 61
EMAIL kontakt@kunsthandel-maass.de
WEB kunsthandel-maass.de

Josef Lebovic Gallery

ADDRESS 103a Anzac Parade
Kensington, Sydney, Australia
NSW 2033
PHONE +61 2 9663 4848
EMAIL josef@joseflebovicgallery.com
WEB joseflebovicgallery.com

Joseph Bellows Gallery*

ADDRESS 7661 Girard Avenue
La Jolla, CA 92037
PHONE 858-456-5620
EMAIL info@josephbellows.com
WEB josephbellows.com

Kathleen Ewing Gallery

ADDRESS	3254 Tradition Circle
	Mt. Pleasant, SC 29466
PHONE	202-812-9830
EMAIL	ewingal@aol.com

Keith de Lellis Gallery*

ADDRESS	41 East 57th Street
	Suite 703
	New York, NY 10022
PHONE	212-327-1482
EMAIL	keith@keithdelellisgallery.com
WEB	keithdelellisgallery.com

Kicken Berlin

ADDRESS	Kaiserdamm 118
	Berlin, Germany 14057
PHONE	+49 30 288 77 882
EMAIL	kicken@kicken-gallery.com
WEB	kicken-gallery.com

L. Parker Stephenson Photographs*

ADDRESS	764 Madison Avenue
	New York, NY 10065
PHONE	212-517-8700
EMAIL	info@lparkerstephenson.com
WEB	lparkerstephenson.com

Laurence Miller Gallery*

ADDRESS	521 West 26th Street
	5th Floor
	New York, NY 10001
PHONE	212-397-3930
EMAIL	contact@laurencemillergallery.com
WEB	laurencemillergallery.com

Lee Gallery*

ADDRESS	9 Mount Vernon Street
	Winchester, MA 01890
PHONE	781-729-7445
EMAIL	info@leegallery.com
WEB	leegallery.com

Lee Marks Fine Art

ADDRESS	2208 East 350 North
	Shelbyville, IN 46176
PHONE	317-696-3324
EMAIL	lee@leemarksfineart.com
WEB	leemarksfineart.com

Les Douches La Galerie

ADDRESS	5 Rue Legouvé
	Paris, France 75010
PHONE	+33 (0)9 54 66 68 85
EMAIL	contact@lesdoucheslagalerie.com
WEB	lesdoucheslagalerie.com

Lisa Sette Gallery

ADDRESS	210 East Catalina Drive
	Phoenix, AZ 85012
PHONE	480-990-7342
EMAIL	sette@lisasettegallery.com
WEB	lisasettegallery.com

Lumina Gallery

ADDRESS	Thomas Heftyes Gate 62A
	Oslo, Norway 00267
PHONE	+47 951 03 161
EMAIL	info@luminagallery.no
WEB	luminagallery.no

2019 Membership Directory

M+B

ADDRESS 612 North Almont Drive
Los Angeles, CA 90069
PHONE 310-550-0050
EMAIL info@mbart.com
WEB mbart.com

MEM, Inc.*

ADDRESS NADiff A/P/A/R/T 3F
1-18-4, Ebisu, Shibuya-ku
Tokyo, Japan 150-0013
PHONE +81-(0)3-6459-3205
EMAIL art@mem-inc.jp
WEB mem-inc.jp

Michael Dawson Gallery

ADDRESS PO Box 39994
Los Angeles, CA 90039
PHONE 213-910-9139
EMAIL michael@michaeldawsongallery.com
WEB michaeldawsongallery.com

Michael Hoppen Gallery*

ADDRESS 3 Jubilee Place
London, United Kingdom
SW3 3TD
PHONE +44 (0)20 7352 3649
EMAIL gallery@michaelhoppengallery.com
WEB michaelhoppengallery.com

Michael Shapiro Photographs*

ADDRESS 606 Post Road East
Westport, CT 06880
PHONE 203-222-3899
EMAIL info@shapirogallery.net
WEB michaelshapirophotographs.com

Monroe Gallery of Photography*

ADDRESS 112 Don Gaspar Avenue
Santa Fe, NM 87501
PHONE 505-992-0800
EMAIL info@monroegallery.com
WEB monroegallery.com

Nicholas Metivier Gallery

ADDRESS 451 King Street West
Toronto, ON Canada
M5V 1K4
PHONE 416-205-9000
EMAIL info@metiviergallery.com
WEB metiviergallery.com

Obscura Gallery

ADDRESS 1405 Paseo de Peralta
Santa Fe, NM 87505
PHONE 505-577-6708
EMAIL info@obscuragallery.net
WEB obscuragallery.net

only photography*

ADDRESS Niebuhrstraße. 78
Berlin, Germany 10629
PHONE +49-30-847 20 291
EMAIL info@only-photography.com
WEB only-photography.com

Pace/MacGill Gallery

ADDRESS 32 East 57th Street
9th Floor
New York, NY 10022
PHONE 212-759-7999
EMAIL info@pacemacgill.com
WEB pacemacgill.com

Paci Contemporary

ADDRESS   Via Trieste 48
          Brescia, Italy 25121
PHONE   +39 0302906352
EMAIL   info@pacicontemporary.com
WEB   pacicontemporary.com

Paul M. Hertzmann, Inc.*

ADDRESS   PO Box 40447
          San Francisco, CA 94140
PHONE   415-626-2677
EMAIL   pmhi@hertzmann.net
WEB   hertzmann.net

PDNB Gallery*

ADDRESS   154 Glass Street
          Suite 104
          Dallas, TX 75207
PHONE   214-969-1852
EMAIL   info@pdnbgallery.com
WEB   pdnbgallery.com

Peter Fetterman Gallery*

ADDRESS   2525 Michigan Avenue
          Santa Monica, CA 90404
PHONE   310-453-6463
EMAIL   info@peterfetterman.com
WEB   peterfetterman.com

PGI*

ADDRESS   TKB Building. 3F 2-3-4
          Higashiazabu, Minato-ku
          Tokyo, Japan 106-0044
PHONE   +81 3-5114-7935
EMAIL   info-e@pgi.ac
WEB   pgi.ac/en

Photographica FineArt Gallery

ADDRESS   Via Cantonale 9
          Lugano, Switzerland 06901
PHONE   +4191 9239675
EMAIL   mail@photographicafineart.com
WEB   photographicafineart.com

Richard Moore Photographs*

ADDRESS   PO Box 16245
          Oakland, CA 94610
PHONE   510-271-0149
EMAIL   info@richardmoorephoto.com
WEB   richardmoorephoto.com

Rick Wester Fine Art, Inc.*

ADDRESS   526 West 26th Street
          Suite 417
          New York, NY 10001
PHONE   212-255-5560
EMAIL   rwfa@rickwesterfineart.com
WEB   rickwesterfineart.com

Robert Burge/20th Century Photographs, Ltd.

ADDRESS   435 East 57th Street
          Suite 16D
          New York, NY 10022
PHONE   212-838-4005
EMAIL   antiques@yaleburge.com
WEB   yaleburge.com

Robert Klein Gallery*

ADDRESS   38 Newbury Street
          Boston, MA 02116
PHONE   617-267-7997
EMAIL   inquiry@robertkleingallery.com
WEB   robertkleingallery.com

2019 Membership Directory

Robert Koch Gallery*

ADDRESS 49 Geary Street
5th Floor
San Francisco, CA 94108
PHONE 415-421-0122
EMAIL info@kochgallery.com
WEB kochgallery.com

Robert Mann Gallery*

ADDRESS 525 West 26th Street
2nd Floor
New York, NY 10001
PHONE 212-989-7600
EMAIL mail@robertmann.com
WEB robertmann.com

Robert Morat Galerie

ADDRESS Linienstrasse 107
Berlin, Germany 10115
PHONE +49 30 25209358
EMAIL kontakt@robertmorat.de
WEB robertmorat.de

Rolf Art*

ADDRESS Esmeralda 1353
Buenos Aires, Argentina
C1007ABS
PHONE +54 11 4326-3679
EMAIL info@rolfart.com.ar
WEB rolfart.com.ar

Scheinbaum & Russek, Ltd.

ADDRESS 369 Montezuma #345
Santa Fe, NM 87501
PHONE 505-988-5116
EMAIL srltd@photographydealers.com
WEB photographydealers.com

Scott Nichols Gallery*

ADDRESS 49 Geary Street
Suite 415
San Francisco, CA 94108
PHONE 415-788-4641
EMAIL info@scottnicholsgallery.com
WEB scottnicholsgallery.com

Sous Les Etoiles Gallery*

ADDRESS 100 Crosby Street
Suite 603
New York, NY 10012
PHONE 212-966-0796
EMAIL info@souslesetoilesgallery.net
WEB souslesetoilesgallery.net

Staley-Wise Gallery*

ADDRESS 100 Crosby Street
Suite 305
New York, NY 10012
PHONE 212-966-6223
EMAIL photo@staleywise.com
WEB staleywise.com

Stephen Bulger Gallery*

ADDRESS 1356 Dundas Street West
Toronto, ON, Canada
M6J 1Y2
PHONE 416-504-0575
EMAIL info@bulgergallery.com
WEB bulgergallery.com

Stephen Daiter Gallery*

ADDRESS 230 West Superior Street
4th Floor
Chicago, IL 60654
PHONE 312-787-3350
EMAIL info@stephendaitergallery.com
WEB stephendaitergallery.com

Taka Ishii Gallery

ADDRESS 6-5-24 3F Roppongi Minato-ku
Tokyo, Japan 106-0032
PHONE +81 (0) 3 6434 7010
EMAIL tig@takaishiigallery.com
WEB takaishiigallery.com

Throckmorton Fine Art*

ADDRESS 145 East 57th Street, 3rd Floor
New York, NY 10022
PHONE 212-223-1059
EMAIL info@throckmorton-nyc.com
WEB throckmorton-nyc.com

Utópica*

ADDRESS Rua Rodésia 26
São Paulo, Brazil 05435020
PHONE (55-11) 3037-7349
EMAIL info@utopica.photography
WEB utopica.photography

Wach Gallery

ADDRESS 31860 Walker Road
Avon Lake, OH 44012
PHONE 440-933-2780
EMAIL mail@wachgallery.com
WEB wachgallery.com

Weinstein Hammons Gallery*

ADDRESS 908 West 46th Street
Minneapolis, MN 55419
PHONE 612-822-1722
EMAIL info@weinsteinhammons.com
WEB weinsteinhammons.com

Weston Gallery, Inc.

ADDRESS 6th Avenue and Delores
Carmel, CA 93921
PHONE 831-624-4453
EMAIL info@westongallery.com
WEB westongallery.com

William L. Schaeffer Photographic Works of Art*

ADDRESS PO Box 296
Chester, CT 06412
PHONE 860-526-3870
EMAIL wmls@me.com
WEB williamlschaeffer.com

Winter Works on Paper*

ADDRESS 167 North 9th Street
Apartment 11
Brooklyn, NY 11211
PHONE 718-599-0910
EMAIL winterworks@verizon.net
WEB winterworksonpaper.com

Yancey Richardson Gallery*

ADDRESS 525 West 22nd Street
New York, NY 10011
PHONE 646-230-9610
EMAIL info@yanceyrichardson.com
WEB yanceyrichardson.com

IX. Book Dealers, Publishers, and Photography-Related Organizations

Book Dealers, Publishers, and Photography-Related Organizations

The Photography Show features a section of the exhibition floor dedicated to book dealers, publishers, and photography-related organizations.

10×10 Photobooks, New York, NY

21st Editions, South Dennis, MA

AKIO NAGASAWA Gallery | Publishing, Tokyo, Japan

American Photography Archives Group, APAG, New York, NY

Aperture Foundation, New York, NY

Artbook Bookstore, New York, NY

Benrido Graphics, Kyoto, Japan

Brilliant Graphics, Exton, PA

Candor Arts, Chicago, IL

Citizen Editions, Brooklyn, NY

Conveyor Editions, Jersey City, NJ

DAMIANI, Bologna, Italy

Daylight Books, Durham, SC

Dust Collective, Stow, MA

GOST Books, London, United Kingdom

Harper's Books, East Hampton, NY

KGP – Kris Graves Projects, Long Island City, NY

KOMIYAMA TOKYO, Chiyoda-ku, Tokyo, Japan

L'Artiere, Bologna, Italy

Light Work, Syracuse, NY

MACK, London, United Kingdom

Minor Matters Books, Seattle, WA

Nazraeli Press, Paso Robles, CA

photo-eye, Santa Fe, NM

photograph magazine, New York, NY

Saint Lucy Books, Baltimore, MD

STANLEY/BARKER, London, United Kingdom

SUPER LABO, Kanagawa, Japan

TBW Books, Oakland, CA

The Classic, Arnaville, France

TIS Books, Brooklyn, NY

Yoffy Press, Atlanta, GA

Zatara Press, Richmond, VA

Alan Klotz Gallery
AIPAD Member

19th-, 20th-, 21st-Century, Vintage, Contemporary, and Modern Photography and Mixed Media

In our 42nd year in business. We are unusual in that we represent all three centuries of photographic output. We do appraisals, act as auction agents, and offer collector seminars.

ADDRESS   740 West End Avenue, Suite #52, New York, NY 10025

PHONE   212-741-4764

EMAIL   info@klotzgallery.com

WEB   www.klotzgallery.com

STAFF   Alan Klotz, Gabrielle Hollender, Sarah Stewart

HOURS   Wednesday-Friday, 10-6, and By Appointment

ARTISTS   Eugène Atget, A. Aubrey Bodine, Margaret Bourke-White, Harry Callahan, Julia M. Cameron, Edward Curtis, Peter Henry Emerson, Frederick H. Evans, Walker Evans, Robert Frank, Lewis Hine, Irving Penn, Tony Ray-Jones, Theodore Roszak, Arthur Rothstein, August Salzmann, Aaron Siskind, Josef Sudek, E&B Weston, Minor White

Julius Shulman
Case house #22, 1960
Gelatin silver print, 20 × 16 in. print on 24 × 20 in. mount
Signed and dated on verso. Framed in a natural wood frame. This image shows Pierre Koenig's Stahl House, a glass-enclosed Hollywood Hills home with a breathtaking view of Los Angeles. It is one of 36 Case Study Houses that were part of an architectural experiment extolling the virtues of modernist theory and industrial materials, mostly shot by Shulman.

708

Arnika Dawkins Gallery Photographic Fine Art

AIPAD Member

Contemporary Photography

Arnika Dawkins Gallery is devoted to presenting fine art from both emerging and established photographers, specializing in images by African Americans and of African Americans.

ADDRESS	4600 Cascade Road, Atlanta, GA 30331
PHONE	404-333-0312
EMAIL	agd@adawkinsgallery.com
WEB	www.adawkinsgallery.com
STAFF	Arnika Dawkins, Rebecca Morgan
HOURS	Tuesday-Friday, 10-4, and By Appointment
ARTISTS	Allen Cooley, Marlene Hawthrone, Ervin A. Johnson, Builder Levy, Jeanine Michna-Bales, Shoccara Marcus, Gordon Parks, Keris Salmon, Aline Smithson

Ervin A. Johnson
Ashli, 2016
Photographic mixed media, 52 × 42 in.
Edition of 1

Atlas Gallery

310

AIPAD Member

20th-, 21st-Century, Vintage, Contemporary, and Modern Photography

Based in the heart of London, Atlas Gallery was founded in 1994 and is one of the foremost galleries in London dealing exclusively in fine art photography.

ADDRESS 49 Dorset Street, London, United Kingdom W1U 7NF

PHONE +44 (0)20 7224 4192

EMAIL info@atlasgallery.com

WEB www.atlasgallery.com

STAFF Ben Burdett, Caterina Mestrovich, Francesca Cronan

HOURS Weekdays, 10-6, Saturday, 11-5

ARTISTS Nick Brandt, Jimmy Nelson, Niko Luoma, Andreas Gefeller, Irving Penn, Bill Brandt, Kacper Kowalski, Steve Schapiro, Frauke Eigen, Richard Caldicott, Chirs Simpson, Gered Mankowitz, John Messinger, Marc Riboud, René Burri, Ernst Haas, Arthur Elgort, LIFE Picture Archive, David Drebin, Floris Neusüss

Chris Simpson
Allee des Baobabs, Madagascar, 1997
Archival pigment print, 44 × 44 in.
Edition of 10
© Chris Simpson, Courtesy of Atlas Gallery

703

Augusta Edwards Fine Art
AIPAD Member

20th-, 21st-Century, Vintage, Contemporary, and Modern Photography
Specializing in classical 20th-century and contemporary fine art photography.

ADDRESS 61 Willow Walk, First Floor, London, United Kingdom SE1 5SF

PHONE +44 20 7064 1070

EMAIL info@augustaedwards.com

WEB www.augustaedwards.com

STAFF Augusta Edwards

HOURS By Appointment

ARTISTS Cecil Beaton, Henri Cartier-Bresson, Geraldo de Barros, Elliott Erwitt, Thomaz Farkas, Mario Fonseca, Martine Franck, Stuart Franklin, Gaspar Gasparian, Heinz Hajek-Halke, Chris Killip, Karen Knorr, Josef Koudelka, Marketa Luskacova, Genevieve Naylor, Norman Parkinson, Graham Smith, Mauricio Valenzuela, Tom Wood, Marcos Zegers

Karen Knorr
In the mood for love, 2018
© Karen Knorr
Courtesy of Augusta Edwards Fine Art

207

Barry Singer Gallery

AIPAD Member

20th- and 21st-Century Photography and Mixed Media

Barry Singer Gallery specializes in vintage prints by Photo League and other photographers of the human condition.

ADDRESS	PO Box 2658, Petaluma, CA 94953
PHONE	707-781-3200
EMAIL	gretchen@singergallery.com
WEB	www.singergallery.com
STAFF	Barry Singer, Gretchen Singer
HOURS	By Appointment
ARTISTS	Eugène Atget, John Baldessari, Roger Ballon, Robert Frank, Dave Heath, Robert Heinecken, Ken Josephson, Barry Kite, Rebecca Lepkoff, Luis G. Palma, George Rodger, Rae Russel, Joe Schwartz, W. Eugene Smith, Lou Stoumen, Edmund Teske, Lloyd Ullberg, Weegee, Brett Weston

W. Eugene Smith
The Walk to Paradise Garden,
1946/60s
Early gelatin silver print
11 15/16 × 10 1/4 in.

baudoin lebon gallery

AIPAD Member

20th-, 21st-Century, Vintage, and Contemporary Photography

For 40 years, baudoin lebon has shown in his artistic choices an obvious individuality without any consideration of comfort or conformity, and a wide open state of mind.

ADDRESS 8 rue Charles-François Dupuis, Paris, France 75003

PHONE +33 1 42 72 09 10

EMAIL info@baudoin-lebon.com

WEB www.baudoin-lebon.com

STAFF Baudoin Lebon, Judith Peyrat, Caroline Lescure, Fabienne Besnard

HOURS Tuesday-Saturday, 11-7

ARTISTS Patrick Bailly-Maitre-Grand, Mathieu Bernard-Reymond, Christian Courrèges, Juliette Andrea-Elie, Franco Fontana, Dorian François, Ayana V. Jackson, Peter Knapp, Robert Mapplethorpe, Lisette Model, Rafael Navarro, Antoine Poupel, Joel-Peter Witkin

Joel-Peter Witkin
Adam and Eve, Shanghai,
2015
Silver print, mixed media
37.7 × 49 cm.
Edition 1/12
© Joel-Peter Witkin
Courtesy of baudoin lebon

211 BOCCARA ART

21st-Century, Contemporary, and Modern Photography, Mixed Media, and Digital Pictorial Photography

BOCCARA ART is a Modern and Contemporary Art Gallery.

ADDRESS	130 West 56th Street, 5M, New York, NY 10019 (office and exhibitions by appointment)
	198 24th Street, Brooklyn, New York, NY 11232 (gallery)
PHONE	646-339-2199, 347-799-1800
EMAIL	ny@boccara-art.com
WEB	www.boccara-art.com
STAFF	Wenxia Chen, Fu Wenjun, Gina Ardani, Zang, Liubov Belousova, Matthew Barash
HOURS	Daily, 11-6
ARTISTS	Fu Wenjun, Hyun Ae Kang, Simone Pheulpin, Benjamin Shine, Chu Teh Chun, Anton Smit, Gianfranco Meggiato, Jim Dine, Joan Miro, Jules Olitski, Leon Zack, Krista Kim, Manolo Valdes, Monique Frydman, Patrick Laroche, Roy Lichtenstein, Wang Keping, Sonia Delaunay, Andy Warhol, Xavier Magali

Fu Wenjun
Red Cherry, 2017/18
Digital pictorial photography, 40 × 40 in.
Unique

500

Bruce Silverstein Gallery
AIPAD Member

19th-, 20th-, 21st-Century, Vintage, Contemporary, and Modern Photography and Mixed Media

Bruce Silverstein Gallery's principal focus is the representation of an international roster of contemporary artists as well as established artists of great influence.

ADDRESS	529 West 20th Street, 3rd Floor, New York, NY 10011
PHONE	212-627-3930
EMAIL	inquiries@brucesilverstein.com
WEB	www.brucesilverstein.com
STAFF	Bruce Silverstein, Elizabeth Eichholz Yoches, Frances Jakubek, Kathleen O'Brien
HOURS	Tuesday-Saturday, 10-6
ARTISTS	Constantin Brâncuși, Mishka Henner, Todd Hido, Nicolai Howalt, André Kertész, Alfred Leslie, René Magritte, Shinichi Maruyama, Man Ray, Lisette Model, Barbara Morgan, Frank Paulin, Larry Silver, Aaron Siskind, Keith A. Smith, Rosalind Fox Solomon, Frederick Sommer, Trine Søndergaard, Brea Souders, Marjan Teeuwen

Marjan Teeuwen
Verwoest Huis Gaza 10, 2016
© Marjan Teeuwen, Courtesy of Bruce Silverstein Gallery

Bryce Wolkowitz Gallery

301

AIPAD Member

Contemporary Photography

Since its founding in 2002, Bryce Wolkowitz Gallery has made a major commitment to representing artists who are exploring the intersection of art and technology.

ADDRESS 505 West 24th Street, New York, NY 10011

PHONE 212-243-8830

EMAIL info@brycewolkowitz.com

WEB www.brycewolkowitz.com

STAFF Bryce Wolkowitz, Amanda Bhalla Wilkes, Andrew Wingert, Samantha Coven, David Price, Sarah McHugh

HOURS Tuesday-Saturday, 10-6

ARTISTS Yorgo Alexopoulos, Edward Burtynsky, Jim Campbell, Robert Currie, Oliver Jeffers, Airan Kang, Niko Luoma, Jimmy Nelson, Sohei Nishino, José Parlá, Alan Rath, Evan Robarts, Paula Scher, Cortis & Sonderegger, Wang Ningde, Stephen Wilkes

Niko Luoma
Self-titled Adaptation of 'Peter getting out of Nick's Pool' (1966) Version I, 2018
Archival pigment print
72 × 61 in.
Edition of 6 + 2 Artist Proofs

Candela Gallery

Contemporary Photography

Established in 2010, Candela Gallery is located in Richmond, Virginia, and is devoted exclusively to exhibiting contemporary fine art photography.

ADDRESS	214 West Broad Street, Richmond, VA 23220
PHONE	804-225-5527
EMAIL	info@candelabooks.com
WEB	www.candelabooks.com
STAFF	Gordon Stettinius, Ashby Nickerson
HOURS	Tuesday-Friday, 11-5, and Saturday, 1-5
ARTISTS	Morgan Ashcom, Sheila Pree Bright, Linda Connor, Courtney Johnson, Chirs McCaw, Anne Arden McDonald, Andreas Rentsch, Kahn & Selesnick, Maggie Taylor, Paul Thulin, Louviere + Vanessa, Harrison Walker, Susan Worsham, Willie Anne Wright

Paul Thulin
At the Right Hand of God, 2013
Archival pigment print, 30 × 24 in.
Edition of 7 + 2 Artist Proofs

Catherine Couturier Gallery

AIPAD Member

20th-Century, Vintage, and Contemporary Photography

Catherine Couturier Gallery is located in Houston, Texas and specializes in classic 20th-century photography and contemporary work of the highest quality.

ADDRESS	2635 Colquitt Street, Houston, TX 77098
PHONE	713-524-5070
EMAIL	gallery@catherinecouturier.com
WEB	www.catherinecouturier.com
STAFF	Catherine Couturier, Ileana Yordan
HOURS	Tuesday-Saturday, 10-5
ARTISTS	Renate Aller, Keith Carter, Elliott Erwitt, André Kertész, Maggie Taylor, Brett Weston, Paul Caponigro, Michael Kenna, Ray Metzker, Henri Cartier-Bresson

Ray Metzker
Philadelphia, 1964

Catherine Edelman Gallery
AIPAD Member

304

Contemporary Photography and Mixed Media
Contemporary photography and mixed media photo-based work with an emphasis on educational programming.

ADDRESS	1637 West Chicago Avenue, Chicago, IL 60622
PHONE	312-266-2350
EMAIL	info@edelmangallery.com
WEB	www.edelmangallery.com
STAFF	Catherine Edelman, Juli Lowe, Tim Campos
HOURS	Tuesday-Saturday, 10-5:30
ARTISTS	Daniel Beltrá, Marina Black, Julie Blackmon, Clarissa Bonet, Kate Breakey, Jess T. Dugan, Elizabeth Ernst, Dan Estabrook, Terry Evans, Garrett O. Hansen, Omar Imam, Michael Kenna, Michael Koerner, Ysabel LeMay, Sandro Miller, Laurent Millet, Robert & Shana ParkeHarrison, Gregory Scott, Joel-Peter Witkin

'He used to electrocute my penis. but then, happily, the tormentor became a fellow prisoner. Revenge was a must.'

Omar Imam
Untitled, [electrocute my penis], 2017
Pigment print, 12 × 17 in. & 18 × 24 in.
Edition of 8 & 6 with 2 Artist Proofs, © Omar Imam

Charles Isaacs Photographs, Inc.
AIPAD Member

19th-, 20th-Century, Vintage, and Modern Photography
Since 1980, we have specialized in vintage photographs of the 19th and 20th centuries.

ADDRESS	25 West 54th Street, Suite 5CD, New York, NY 10019
PHONE	212-957-3238
EMAIL	cti@charlesisaacs.com
WEB	www.charlesisaacs.com
STAFF	Charles Isaacs, Carol Nigro, PhD, Gregory Leroy
HOURS	By Appointment
ARTISTS	Eugène Atget, Manuel Álvarez Bravo, Lola Álvarez Bravo, Adolphe Braun, Julia M. Cameron, Giacomo Caneva, Laura Gilpin, Katy Horna, Bernice Kolko, Clarence J. Laughlin, Gustave Le Gray, Charles Marville, Timothy O'Sullivan, Antonio Reynoso, Auguste Salzmann, Armando Salas Portugal, Jose Maria Sert, William H.F. Talbot, Linnaeus Tripe, Edward Weston

Antonio Reynoso
Soledad / Sadness, 1942
Vintage silver print, titled and
dated, 9 3/16 × 7 1/2 in.
© Estate of the artist

ClampArt

AIPAD Member

20th-, 21st-Century, Vintage, Contemporary, and Modern Photography and Mixed Media

Established in 2000, ClampArt represents a wide range of emerging and mid-career artists of all media with a specialization in photography.

ADDRESS 247 West 29th Street, Ground Floor, New York, NY 10001

PHONE 646-230-0020

EMAIL info@clampart.com

WEB www.clampart.com

STAFF Brian Paul Clamp, Raechel McCarthy, Sullivan Gardner, Mickey Aloisio

HOURS Tuesday-Saturday, 10-6

ARTISTS Bill Armstrong, Olaf Otto Becker, Brian Buckley, Jesse Burke, Aziz + Cucher, Robert Calafiore, Jen Davis, Frances F. Denny, Adam Ekberg, Brian Finke, Jill Greenberg, Daniel Handal, Michael Massaia, Pipo Nguyen-duy, Lori Nix/Kathleen Gerber, Lissa Rivera, Zack Seckler, Manjari Sharma, Marc Yankus, Ion Zupcu

Olaf Otto Becker
Primary Forest 18, Roots, Malaysia, 10/2012, 2012
Archival pigment print
© Olaf Otto Becker

Contemporary Works/Vintage Works

AIPAD Member

19th-, 20th-, 21st-Century, Vintage, Contemporary, and Modern Photography and Mixed Media

World's largest private dealer selling master 19th-, 20th-, and 21st-century images from an inventory of 5,000+ international photos, emphasizing American, French, and English.

ADDRESS	258 Inverness Circle, Chalfont, PA 18914
PHONE	215-822-5662
EMAIL	info@vintageworks.net
WEB	www.vintageworks.net
STAFF	Alex Novak, Marthe Smith
HOURS	By Appointment
ARTISTS	Laure Albin-Guillot, Charles Aubry, Hippolyte Bayard, Hans Bellmer, Erwin Blumenfeld, Brassaï, Harry Callahan, Julia M. Cameron, Henri Cartier-Bresson, Robert Doisneau, Robert Frank, John B. Greene, André Kertész, Heinrich Kuhn, Gustave Le Gray, Man Ray, Charles Marville, Charles Negre, Irving Penn, Edward Weston

Nadar (and painted by E. Vieusseux)
Charles-Albert Costa de Beauregard in Military Uniform with Sword, 1871
Painted albumen print from enlarged wet plate negative, 21 5/8 × 17 11/16 in.
(550 × 450 mm)
Unique

Contemporary Photography

Representing early career and established artists with a focus on contemporary photography and new approaches to the medium.

ADDRESS	1350 Abbot Kinney Boulevard, Venice, CA 90291
PHONE	323-253-2255
EMAIL	info@desotogallery.com
WEB	www.desotogallery.com
STAFF	Shelley De Soto, Mateo De Soto
HOURS	By Appointment
ARTISTS	Alma Haser, Connie Samaras, Denis Darzacq, Ivan Forde, Judy Gelles, Laura Plageman, Ramona Rosales, Osamu Yokonami

Ivan Forde
Three Rivers, 2018
Blueprint on rice paper, 25 × 50 in.
Unique
© Ivan Forde

Deborah Bell Photographs

AIPAD Member

20th-, 21st-Century, Vintage, and Modern Photography

Vintage photographs from the 20th and 21st centuries.

ADDRESS	16 East 71st Street, Suite 1D, 4th Floor, New York, NY 10021
PHONE	212-249-9400
EMAIL	info@deborahbellphotographs.com
WEB	www.deborahbellphotographs.com
STAFF	Deborah Bell
HOURS	Wednesday-Saturday, 11-6
ARTISTS	Erwin Blumenfeld, Mariana Cook, Louis Faurer, G.P. Fieret, Edward Grazda, Sid Kaplan, Rose Mandel, Ann Parker, Susan Paulsen, Gösta Peterson, Edward Ranney, Marcia Resnick, Ringl + Pit, August Sander, William Silano, Deborah Turbeville, Edward Wallowitch, Minor White

Deborah Turbeville
Montova, Italy (Isabelle Weingarten), 1977
Diptych of gelatin silver prints, 11 × 19 in. (27.9 × 48.3 cm.)
© The Deborah Turbeville Foundation

Edwynn Houk Gallery

AIPAD Member

20th-, 21st-Century, Vintage, and Contemporary Photography

Edwynn Houk Gallery specializes in vintage photographs from 1917-1939 and represents a select group of leading contemporary photographers.

ADDRESS	745 Fifth Avenue, New York, NY 10151
PHONE	212-750-7070
EMAIL	info@houkgallery.com
WEB	www.houkgallery.com
STAFF	Edwynn Houk, Julie Castellano, Alexis Dean, Julia Hartshorn, Veronica Houk, Tess Vinnedge, Christian Houk, Benjamin Blumberg
HOURS	Tuesday-Saturday, 11-6
ARTISTS	Lillian Bassman, Valérie Belin, Erwin Blumenfeld, Nick Brandt, Sebastiaan Bremer, Lynn Davis, Michael Eastman, Lalla Essaydi, Robert Frank, André Kertész, David Maisel, Sally Mann, László Moholy-Nagy, Abelardo Morell, Vik Muniz, Matthew Pillsbury, Man Ray, Stephen Shore, Alfred Stieglitz, Paolo Ventura

Valérie Belin
White Narcissus in Orange (Colour Wonder), 2018
Archival pigment print,
51 5/8 × 41 3/8 in.
Edition of 25, © Valérie Belin
Courtesy of the artist and Edwynn Houk Gallery, New York

907 Elizabeth Houston Gallery

19th-, 20th-, 21st-Century, Vintage, Conteporary, and Modern Photography

Elizabeth Houston Gallery represents a wide range of emerging and mid-career artists of all media, with a specialization in photography.

ADDRESS 190 Orchard Street, New York, NY 10002

PHONE 646-918-6462

EMAIL info@elizabethhoustongallery.com

WEB www.elizabethhoustongallery.com

STAFF Elizabeth Houston, Alexander Bingham, Melanie Lauer

HOURS Wednesday-Sunday, 11-6

ARTISTS Daniel W. Coburn, Nico Krijno, Mark Lyon, Amy Finkelstein, Andy Mattern, Melanie Willhide, John Cyr, Aaron Siskind, Larry Clark, Roger Ballen, Louis Faurer, Luis González Palma, Josef Sudek, Edmund Teske, Weegee

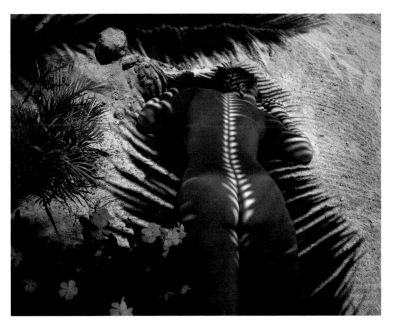

Daniel W. Coburn
Untitled, 2017
Archival pigment print, 32 × 40 in.

Etherton Gallery

AIPAD Member

Vintage, Contemporary, and Modern Photography

Etherton Gallery specializes in post-World War II American photography and provides a platform for contemporary artists changing the course of the medium since 1981.

ADDRESS	135 South Sixth Avenue, Tucson, AZ 85701
PHONE	520-624-7370
EMAIL	info@ethertongallery.com
WEB	www.ethertongallery.com
STAFF	Terry Etherton, Hannah Glasston, Daphne Srinivasan, Lisa Roden, Shannon Smith
HOURS	Tuesday-Saturday, 11-5
ARTISTS	Ansel Adams, Diane Arbus, Roger Ballen, Manuel Álvarez Bravo, Harry Callahan, Elliott Erwitt, Robert Frank, Lee Friedlander, Ralph Gibson, Emmet Gowin, Graciela Iturbide, Mark Klett, Danny Lyon, Richard Misrach, Rodrigo Moya, W. Eugene Smith, Frederick Sommer, Alex Webb, Joel-Peter Witkin, Masao Yamamoto

Danny Lyon
Clarksdale, Mississippi, 1963
Vintage gelatin silver print, 6 3/8 × 9 5/8 in.
© Danny Lyon/Magnum Photos, Courtesy of Etherton Gallery, Tucson

Fahey/Klein Gallery

AIPAD Member

20th-, 21st-Century, Vintage, Contemporary, and Modern Photography

The Fahey/Klein Gallery is devoted to the enhancement of the public's appreciation of the medium of photography through the exhibition and sale of fine art photography.

ADDRESS	148 North La Brea Avenue, Los Angeles, CA 90036
PHONE	323-934-2250
EMAIL	contact@faheykleingallery.com
WEB	www.faheykleingallery.com
STAFF	David Fahey, Anne Fahey, Nicholas Fahey, Marco Paez, Nick Cloutman, Heather Cronan, Brian Moreland
HOURS	Tuesday-Saturday, 10-6
ARTISTS	Janette Beckman, Amanda Charchian, Steven Arnold, Brendan Pattengale, Miles Aldridge, Dennis Hopper, Alex Stoddard, Peter Beard, Steve Schapiro

Janette Beckman
CEY, Keith 2.0, 1985/2014
Archival pigment print, 60 × 40 in.
Edition of 8 © Janette Beckman
Courtesy of Fahey/Klein Gallery
Also available in 24 × 20 in. and
40 × 30 in.

Flowers Gallery

AIPAD Member

Contemporary Photography

Founded in 1970 by Angela Flowers in the UK, Flowers now has galleries in both the West End and East End of London together with a third gallery space in Chelsea, New York.

ADDRESS 529 West 20th Street, New York, NY 10011

PHONE 212-439-1700

EMAIL newyork@flowersgallery.com

WEB www.flowersgallery.com

STAFF Matthew Flowers, Emily Flowers, Brent Beamon, Rebecca Reeve, Lieve Beumer

HOURS Tuesday-Saturday, 10-6

ARTISTS Boomoon, Michael Benson, Edward Burtynsky, Edmund Clark, Julie Cockburn, Boyd & Evans, Scarlett Hooft Graafland, Nadav Kander, Mona Kuhn, Jason Larkin, Tom Lovelace, Robert Polidori, Simon Roberts, Esther Teichmann, Lorenzo Vitturi, Shen Wei, Michael Wolf

Julie Cockburn
It's Complicated 5, 2017
Screenprint on Giclee print on Hahnemühle Rag, 54 3/4 × 40 in. (139 × 101.5 cm.)
Unique © Julie Cockburn

Fraenkel Gallery

AIPAD Member

19th-, 20th-, and 21st-Century Photography
Founded in 1979.

ADDRESS	49 Geary Street, Fourth Floor, San Francisco, CA 94108
PHONE	415-981-2661
EMAIL	mail@fraenkelgallery.com
WEB	www.fraenkelgallery.com
STAFF	Jeffrey Fraenkel, Frish Brandt, Amy R. Whiteside, Daphne Palmer
HOURS	Tuesday-Friday, 10:30-5:30, and Saturday, 11-5
ARTISTS	Robert Adams, Diane Arbus, Richard Avedon, Bernd & Hilla Becher, Elisheva Biernoff, Mel Bochner, Sophie Calle, Lee Friedlander, Adam Fuss, Nan Goldin, Katy Grannan, Peter Hujar, Richard Learoyd, Christian Marclay, Ralph Eugene Meatyard, Richard Misrach, Nicholas Nixon, Alec Soth, Hiroshi Sugimoto, Garry Winogrand

Peter Hujar
Sheryl Sutton (I), 1977
Gelatin silver print

Galerie Catherine et André Hug

21st-Century Photography

Since 2000, the Galerie located in the heart of Paris has chosen to present photography for its ability to question reality, explore dreams, and narrate stories.

ADDRESS   40 rue de Seine, Paris, France 75006

PHONE   +33 (1) 607 13 4800

EMAIL   c.hug@orange.fr

WEB   www.galeriehug.com

STAFF   Catherine Hug, André Hug

HOURS   Tuesday-Saturday, 2:30-7

ARTISTS   Reine Paradis, Kourtney Roy, Maroesjka Lavigne, Joni Sternbach, Susan Meiselas, Stuart Franklin, George Tatge, Eric Weeks, Philippe Chancel, Vincent Mercier, Will Adler, Mona Kuhn

Reine Paradis
The Tower, 2018
Archival pigment print, 60 × 42 in.
Edition of 5 + 2 Artist Proofs, © Reine Paradis / Galerie Catherine et André Hug

Galerie f5,6

AIPAD Member

20th-, 21st-Century, Vintage, Contemporary, and Modern Photography

Galerie f5,6 was founded in 2003 in Munich, Germany. We represent established and emerging photographers, exhibit contemporary as well as vintage photography.

ADDRESS   Ludwigstrasse 7, München, Bayern, Germany 80539

PHONE   +49 89 28675167

EMAIL   info@f56.net

WEB   www.f56.net

STAFF   Katrin Weber

HOURS   Wednesday-Friday, 12-6, Saturday, 12-3

ARTISTS   Lillian Bassman, Clara Bahlsen, Olaf Otto Becker, Adolphe Braun, Paul Himmel, Gerry Johansson, Saul Leiter, Ulrich Schmitt, Anne Schwalbe, Tomio Seike, Raghubir Singh, Carl Strüwe, Ed van der Elsken, Hanns Zischler, Helen Levitt, Juliane Eirich

Anne Schwalbe
Wiese LIV, 2018
C-Print

GALERIE FRÉDÉRIC GOT

20th-Century and Contemporary Photography

Galerie GOT is a contemporary art gallery representing many significant international modern artists, through seven galleries in France and one in Montreal.

ADDRESS   35-37 rue de Seine, Paris, France 75006

PHONE   +33 (0) 6 03 68 59 20

EMAIL   gallerygot@gmail.com

WEB   www.fredericgot.com

STAFF   Frédéric Got, Saul Santos, Renaud Lazard

HOURS   Daily, 10:30-9:30

ARTISTS   Harry Benson, Steve McCurry, Annie Leibovitz, Denis Felix, Jacques Le Bescond, Carlos Mata, Tolla Inbar, Hunt Slonem, Peter Hoffer, Peter Zimmermann, Remi Bourquin, Gonzalez Bravo, Andrei Zadorine, Roman Zaslonov

Harry Benson
Beatles. Pillow Fight, 1964
Infused dyes sublimated on aluminium, 106 × 112 cm. (42 × 44 in.)
Edition 14 of 20
© Harry Benson

GALLERY 19/21

AIPAD Member

19th-, 20th-, 21st-Century, Vintage, and Contemporary Photography

European vintage photographs from the 19th and 20th centuries.

ADDRESS	9 Little Harbor Road, Guilford, CT 06437
PHONE	857-991-1822
EMAIL	gallery19th21st@aol.com
WEB	www.gallery19-21.com
STAFF	Roland Baron, Philippe Baron
HOURS	By Appointment
ARTISTS	Eugène Atget, Edouard Boubat, Brassaï, Henri Cartier-Bresson, Frantisek Drtikol, Jean-Baptiste Frénet, Mario Giacomelli, Holics Gyula, Yasuhiro Ishimoto, André Kertész, William Klein, François Kollar, Jacques-Henri Lartigue, Ray Metzker, Daido Moriyama, Shigeru Onishi, Vilem Reichman, Joseph Sudek, Maurice Tabard, Josef Vetrovsky

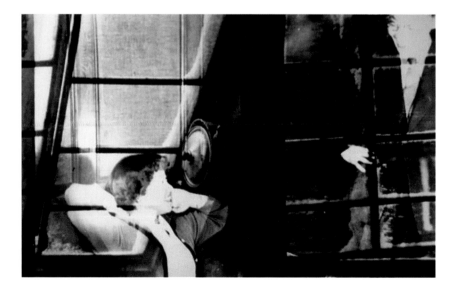

Shigeru Onishi
Japanese (1928-1994), circa 1950
Vintage ferrotyped silver print, 11 1/8 × 7 3/8 in.

Gary Edwards Gallery
AIPAD Member

19th-, 20th-, 21st-Century, Vintage, and Modern Photography

The gallery specializes in early photographs on paper, plus 20th- and 21st-century photographs.

ADDRESS   14 Wolf Swamp Lane, Southampton, NY 11968

PHONE   301-524-0900

EMAIL   garymedwards@mac.com

STAFF   Irene Edwards, Thomas Edwards, Claudia Edwards

HOURS   By Appointment

ARTISTS   James Anderson, Edouard Baldus, Felice Beato, Ernest Benecke, Samuel Bourne, Dimitri Constantine, Maxime DuCamp, Joey Farrell, John B. Greene, Juan Laurent, Charles Nègre, Eugène Piot, Press prints, James Robertson, Ni Rong, Auguste Salzmann, William J. Stillman, William Fox Talbot, Linneus Tripe, Francesca Woodman

Francesca Woodman
Untitled, 1978-80
Vintage gelatin silver print, 4 1/4 × 4 1/4 in.

GILLES PEYROULET & CIE

AIPAD Member

19th-, 20th-, 21st-Century, Vintage, and Contemporary Photography
Established in 1987 in Paris – Fine Vintage and Contemporary Photographs.

ADDRESS	80 rue Quincampoix, Paris, France 75003
PHONE	+33 (0)1 42 78 85 11
EMAIL	contact@galeriepeyroulet.com
WEB	www.galeriepeyroulet.com
STAFF	Dominique Chenivesse, Gilles Peyroulet
HOURS	Tuesday-Saturday, 2-7
ARTISTS	Ladislav Berka, Aenne Biermann, Ilse Bing, Erwin Blumenfeld, Rudy Burckhardt, Claude-Joseph-Désiré Charnay, Charles Clifford, Eugène Cuvelier, John Beasley Greene, Raoul Hausmann, François Kollar, Germaine Krull, Elizabeth Lennard, Mikael Levin, Eli Lotar, Dora Maar, Jean Moral, Sasha Stone, Henri Sauvaire, Raoul Ubac

Clifton L. King
Clara Bow (in *Dangerous Curves*), 1929
Vintage silver gelatin print, 32.8 × 26.5 cm.
Courtesy of Gilles Peyroulet & Cie, Paris
Stamped on the back

Gitterman Gallery

AIPAD Member

19th-, 20th-, 21st-Century, Vintage, Contemporary, and Modern Photography

We specialize in connoisseur-level photographs from a broad range of styles and periods, often championing artists who have been previously overlooked.

ADDRESS	41 East 57th Street, Suite 1103, New York, NY 10022
PHONE	212-734-0868
EMAIL	info@gittermangallery.com
WEB	www.gittermangallery.com
STAFF	Tom Gitterman, John Cowey
HOURS	Tuesday-Saturday, 10-6
ARTISTS	Khalik Allah, Roswell Angier, Adam Bartos, Ferenc Berko, Machiel Botman, Josef Breitenbach, Debbie Fleming Caffery, Lois Conner, Allen Frame, Richard Gordon, Kenneth Josephson, William Larson, Daniel Masclet, Herbert Matter, Roger Mayne, Klea McKenna, Henry Holmes Smith, Jean-Pierre Sudre, Joseph Szabo, Edmund Teske

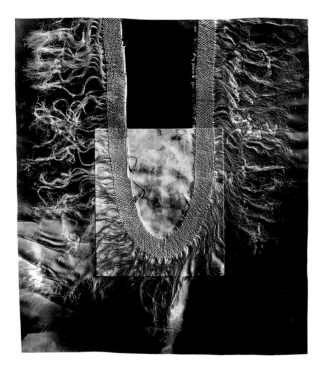

Klea McKenna
Snakes in the Garden (1),
2018
Gelatin silver print;
unique photogram with
impression
39 3/4 × 36 1/2 in.
© Klea McKenna

214

HackelBury Fine Art
AIPAD Member

20th-, 21st-Century, Contemporary, and Modern Photography and Mixed Media

Founded in 1998, HackelBury Fine Art deals in 20th- and 21st-century artworks from a carefully selected stable of artists with a focus on photography.

ADDRESS	4 Launceston Place, London, United Kingdom W8 5RL
PHONE	+44 20 7937 8688
EMAIL	gallery@hackelbury.co.uk
WEB	www.hackelbury.co.uk
STAFF	Marcus Bury, Sascha Hackel, Phil Crook
HOURS	Tuesday-Saturday, 10-5
ARTISTS	Bill Armstrong, Pierre Cordier, Stephen Inggs, Oli Kellett, William Klein, Pascal Kern, Katja Liebmann, Ian McKeever, Garry Fabian Miller, Nadezda Nikolova-Kratzer, Malick Sidibé, Doug and Mike Starn, Alys Tomlinson

Garry Fabian Miller
Almost, 2008-2015
Light, water, Lambda C-print from dye destruction print, 56 × 81 in.
Edition of 3 © Garry Fabian Miller

The Halsted Gallery

AIPAD Member

19th-, 20th-, 21st-Century, Vintage, Contemporary, and Modern Photography

Established in 1969, The Halsted Gallery is the oldest in the country dedicted to the promotion and education of fine art photography

ADDRESS   2235 Cole Street, Birmingham, MI 48009

PHONE   248-792-5487

EMAIL   wendy@halstedgallery.com

WEB   www.halstedgallery.com

STAFF   Wendy Halsted, Julie Smith

HOURS   Tuesday-Saturday, 10-2, and By Appointment

ARTISTS   Ansel Adams, Berenice Abbott, Imogen Cunningham, Ruth Bernhard, Bill Brandt, Wynn Bullock, Robert Capa, Morris Engle, Walker Evans, FH Evans, Yousf Karsh, André Kertész, Michael Kenna, O. Winston Link, Barbara Morgan, Alfred Stieglitz, August Sander, Ralph Steiner, Edward Weston, Carleton Watkins

Walker Evans
Main Street,
Saratoga Springs, 1931
Silver gelatin, 8 × 10 in.

Hans P. Kraus Jr. Inc.
AIPAD Member

19th-, 20th-Century, Vintage, and Contemporary Photography

Hans P. Kraus Jr. Inc., established in New York in 1984, is a dealer in 19th- and early 20th-century photographs.

ADDRESS	962 Park Avenue, New York, NY 10028
PHONE	212-794-2064
EMAIL	info@sunpictures.com
WEB	www.sunpictures.com
STAFF	Hans P. Kraus Jr., Shelley Dowell, Jennifer Wilkinson, Thomas Wood
HOURS	By Appointment
ARTISTS	Eugène Atget, Anna Atkins, Édouard Baldus, Julia Margaret Cameron, Frederick H. Evans, Roger Fenton, Louis-Antoine Froissart, J. B. Greene, Hill & Adamson, Rev. Calvert Jones, Gustave Le Gray, Henri Le Secq, Charles Marville, Charles Nègre, John Ruskin, William Henry Fox Talbot, Félix Teynard, Linnaeus Tripe, Hugo van Werden, Joseph vicomte Vigier, and others

Hugo van Werden
Iron Pilot Boat, 1870s
Albumen print, 24.5 × 34.6 cm.

Henry Feldstein

AIPAD Member

20th-Century and Vintage Photography

Henry Feldstein specializes in vintage 20th-century photography and maintains a large selection of images by Weegee and a large selection of vintage Bettie Page photographs.

ADDRESS	PO Box 398, Forest Hills, NY 11375
PHONE	718-544-3002
EMAIL	henryfe@ix.netcom.com
WEB	www.henryfeldsteinphotographs.com
STAFF	Henry Feldstein
HOURS	By Appointment
ARTISTS	Berenice Abbott, Ansel Adams, Elmer Batters, A. Aubrey Bodine, Brassaï, Hugo Brehme, Wynn Bullock, Larry Clark, Andre De Dienes, Walker Evans, André Kertész, Bettie Page, W. Eugene Smith, Karl Struss, Weegee, Brett Weston, Minor White, Garry Winogrand, Max Yavno, Bunny Yeager

Weegee
The Human Cannonball, 1943
Gelatin silver print, 13 3/8 × 10 in.
© Weegee / International Center of Photography

Holden Luntz Gallery, Inc.

AIPAD Member

20th-, 21st-Century, Contemporary, and Modern Photography

Holden Luntz Gallery exhibits the finest in classic and contemporary American and European photography.

ADDRESS	332 Worth Avenue, Palm Beach, FL 33480
PHONE	561-805-9550
EMAIL	info@holdenluntz.com
WEB	www.holdenluntz.com
STAFF	Holden Luntz, Jodi Luntz, Gabriel Gordon, Jaye Luntz, Roseanna Opper, Cecilia Silva, Mario Lopez Pisani
HOURS	Monday-Saturday, 10-5:30
ARTISTS	Harry Benson, Henri Cartier-Bresson, Elliott Erwitt, Horst P. Horst, Frank Horvat, Karen Knorr, Andre Lichtenberg, Massimo Listri, Michael Massaia, Garry Fabian Miller, David Yarrow, Albert Watson, Brett Weston

Albert Watson
Kate Moss Back II, Marrakech, Morocco,
1993, Printed Later
Archival pigment photograph, 30 × 24 in.
Edition of 25

Howard Greenberg Gallery

AIPAD Member

Vintage, Modern, and Contemporary Photography

The gallery specializes in classic and contemporary photography with an emphasis on photojournalism, European and American Modernism, New York School, and The Photo Secession.

ADDRESS	41 East 57th Street, Suite 1406, New York, NY 10022
PHONE	212-334-0010
EMAIL	info@howardgreenberg.com
WEB	www.howardgreenberg.com
STAFF	Howard Greenberg, Karen Marks, David Peckman, Alicia Colen, Cortney Norman, Morgan Beckwith
HOURS	Tuesday-Saturday, 10-6
ARTISTS	Berenice Abbott, Edward Burtynsky, Henri Cartier-Bresson, Bruce Davidson, František Drtikol, Louis Faurer, Dave Heath, William Klein, Jungjin Lee, Saul Leiter, Vivian Maier, Alex Majoli, Mary Ellen Mark, Ray K. Metzker, Joel Meyerowitz, Arnold Newman, Marvin Newman, Gordon Parks, Steve Schapiro, Paul Strand

Ray K. Metzker
58 CD-4, Chicago,
1958
Gelatin silver,
7 1/2 × 7 3/8 in.
© Estate of Ray K.
Metzker, Courtesy of
Howard Greenberg
Gallery, New York

Huxley-Parlour Gallery

AIPAD Member

20th- and 21st-Century Photography

Huxley-Parlour Gallery was founded in London in 2010. The gallery's exhibition program focuses on photographers who have played a significant role in the history of art.

ADDRESS	3-5 Swallow Street, London, United Kingdom W1B 4DE
PHONE	+44 020 7434 4319
EMAIL	gallery@huxleyparlour.com
WEB	www.huxleyparlour.com
STAFF	Giles Huxley-Parlour, Thea Gregory, Alexandra MacKay, Russell Bruce-Youles, Helen Hayman, Emma Sharples
HOURS	Monday-Saturday, 10-5:30
ARTISTS	Berenice Abbott, Olaf Otto Becker, Valérie Belin, Bruce Davidson, Terence Donovan, Elliott Erwitt, Cig Harvey, Yousuf Karsh, Zhang Kechun, Michael Kenna, Nico Krijno, Jocelyn Lee, Vivian Maier, Steve McCurry, Joel Meyerowitz, Abelardo Morell, Arnold Newman, Martin Parr, Wang Qingsong, Sebastião Salgado

Bruce Gilden
Untitled, New York City, 1978
Silver gelatin print, 16 × 20 in.
Edition of 20 © Bruce Gilden

Hyperion Press, Ltd.

AIPAD Member

20th-, 21st-Century, Vintage, Contemporary, and Modern Photography

Private dealer specializing in vintage and contemporary photographs, limited editions, French, Chinese, and Czech photography.

ADDRESS	200 West 86th Street, New York, NY 10024
PHONE	212-877-2131
EMAIL	hyperionpr@verizon.net
WEB	www.hyperionpressltd.com
STAFF	Monah L. Gettner, Alan Gettner
HOURS	By Appointment
ARTISTS	Hans Bellmer, Edouard Boubat, Bragagia Brothers, Manuel Álvarez Bravo, Henri Cartier-Bresson, Robert Doisneau, Louis Faurer, Ralph Gibson, Horst P. Horst, André Kertész, William Klein, Jacques-Henri Lartigue, Jan Lukas, Danny Lyon, Man Ray, Rene-Jacques, Willy Ronis, Maurice Tabard, Qin Wen, Garry Winogrand

Man Ray
Meret Oppenheim, 1931-32
Gelatin silver contact print on "carte postale" paper, 4 1/2 × 3 1/4 in.
Rue du Val de Grace stamp on verso

IBASHO

AIPAD Member

20th-, 21st-Century, Vintage, Contemporary, and Modern Photography

IBASHO is a gallery in Antwerp, Belgium, specializing in fine art Japanese photography ranging from vintage and earlier works to contemporary photography.

ADDRESS	Tolstraat 67, 2000 Antwerp, Belgium
PHONE	+32 (0)32162028
EMAIL	info@ibashogallery.com
WEB	www.ibashogallery.com
STAFF	Martijn van Pieterson, Annemarie Zethof
HOURS	Friday-Sunday, 2-6, and By Appointment
ARTISTS	Yoshinori Mizutani, Miho Kajioka, Naoyuki Ogino, Toshio Shibata, Motohiro Takeda, Photographer Hal, Albarrán Cabrera, Yoko Ikeda, Kumi Oguro, Casper Faassen, Hideyuki Ishibashi, Ken Kitano, Asako Narahashi, Mikiko Hara, Mika Horie, Tokyo Rumando, Hitoshi Fugo, Hiromi Tsuchida, Yasuhiro Ishimoto, Daido Moriyama

Casper Faassen
Shunji, 2016
Mixed media, 80 × 50 cm.
Edition of 7
© Casper Faassen

Contemporary Photography

In The Gallery is a contemporary art gallery in the centre of Copenhagen, dedicated to showcasing emerging and established artists working predominantly with camera-based art.

ADDRESS	Dronningens Tvaergade 19, Copenhagen, Denmark 1302
PHONE	+45 33 73 11 33
EMAIL	info@inthegallery.com
WEB	www.inthegallery.com
STAFF	Maibritt Rangstrup
HOURS	Wednesday-Friday, 12-5, and Saturday, 11-3
ARTISTS	Jacob Gils, Lea Jessen, Julien Mauve, Carsten Ingemann, Pauline Ballet, Malthe Brandenburg, Stephan Schnedler

Jacob Gils
Frederiksdal #7, 2018
43 × 29 in.
Edition of 6 © Jacob Gils

Jackson Fine Art

AIPAD Member

20th-Century and Contemporary Photography

20th-century and contemporary photography since 1990.

ADDRESS	3115 East Shadowlawn Avenue Northeast, Atlanta, GA 30305
PHONE	404-233-3739
EMAIL	courtney@jacksonfineart.com
WEB	www.jacksonfineart.com
STAFF	Anna Walker Skillman, Courtney Lee Martin
HOURS	Tuesday-Saturday, 10-5
ARTISTS	Gail Albert Halaban, Harry Callahan, John Chiara, William Christenberry, Bruce Davidson, Elliott Erwitt, Thomas Jackson, Mona Kuhn, Erik Madigan Heck, Sally Mann, Andrew Moore, Lyle Owerko, Matthew Pillsbury, Meghann Riepenhoff, Steve Schapiro, Vee Speers, Mark Steinmetz, Ruud Van Empel, Bastiaan Woudt, Masao Yamamoto

Masao Yamamoto
Bonsai #4007, 2018
Silver gelatin print, 20 × 16 in.
Edition of 5 © Masao Yamamoto
Courtesy of Jackson Fine Art

James Hyman Gallery
AIPAD Member

19th-, 20th-, 21st-Century, Vintage, Contemporary, and Modern Photography

James Hyman Gallery was founded in 1999 and aspires to deal in museum-quality fine art and photography of art historical significance.

ADDRESS	PO Box 67698, London, United Kingdom NW11 1NE
PHONE	+44 (0)207 494 3857
EMAIL	info@jameshymangallery.com
WEB	www.jameshymangallery.com
STAFF	James Hyman, David Low, Claire Hyman
HOURS	By Appointment
ARTISTS	Édouard Baldus, Joseph-Philibert Girault de Prangey, André Giroux, Gustave Le Gray, Charles Negre, Ilse Bing, Bill Brandt, Harry Callahan, André Kertész, Linda McCartney, Aaron Siskind, Heather Agyepong, Anna Fox, Ken Grant, Brian Griffin, Bert Hardy, Paul Hill, Homer Sykes, Tony Ray-Jones, Paul Reas

André Kertész
New York (men sitting at base of flag pole), 1938
Enlarged mounted exhibition print, 24 × 20 in.
Unique in this format
© The Estate of André Kertész
Printed for the Venice Biennale in 1963

Joel Soroka Gallery

AIPAD Member

Vintage and Contemporary Photography

20th-century and contemporary photography in Aspen since 1993.

ADDRESS	PO Box 1226, Aspen, CO 81612
PHONE	970-923-4393
EMAIL	joelsorokagallery@gmail.com
WEB	www.joelsorokagallery.com
STAFF	Joel Soroka
HOURS	By Appointment
ARTISTS	Berenice Abbott, John Ahern, Ilse Bing, Frantisek Drtikol, Luis Gonzalez Palma, Samuel Gottscho, Johan Hagemeyer, Cig Harvey, Beatrice Helg, Lewis Hine, Gyorgy Kepes, Man Ray, Ira Martin, Edward Quigley, Lou Stoumen, Josef Sudek, Jindrich Vanek, Brett Weston, Edward Weston

Ilse Bing
Dance School, Frankfurt, 1929
Warm toned gelatin silver print, 3 1/2 × 6 1/2 in.
Mounted to original exhibition mount. Initialed, annotated and dated recto

Jörg Maaß Kunsthandel

AIPAD Member

20th-, 21st-Century, Vintage, Contemporary, and Modern Photography

Established in 1987, Jörg Maaß Kunsthandel specializes in art from the classical modern period as well as in European and American photography from the 1920s to contemporary.

ADDRESS	Rankestraße 24, Berlin, Germany 10789
PHONE	+49 (0)30 211 54 61
EMAIL	kontakt@kunsthandel-maass.de
WEB	www.kunsthandel-maass.de
STAFF	Jörg Maaß, Sabine Maaß, Pia Lenz, Nadine Pfeil, Sonja von Oertzen
HOURS	Monday-Friday, 10-4, and By Appointment
ARTISTS	Robert Adams, Diane Arbus, Ilse Bing, Bill Brandt, Brassaï, Harry Callahan, William Eggleston, Robert Frank, Andreas Feininger, Charles Johnstone, Peter Keetman, Germaine Krull, Gilles Lorin, Annie Leibovitz, Helmut Newton, Gerhard Richter, Tata Ronkholz, Otto Steinert, Alec Soth

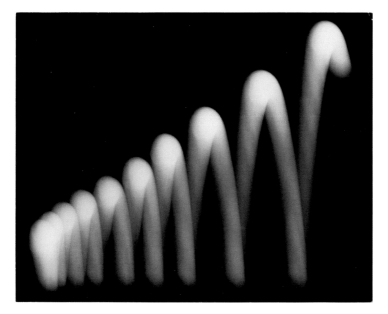

Peter Keetman
Springender Tischtennisball, 1954
Gelatin silver print, 227 × 292 mm.
© Estate Peter Keetman / F.C. Gundlach Foundation

Joseph Bellows Gallery

AIPAD Member

601

20th-Century, Vintage, and Contemporary Photography

Joseph Bellows Gallery supports an inventory of important vintage and contemporary photographs, with a special interest in American work from the 1970s.

ADDRESS	7661 Girard Avenue, La Jolla, CA 92037
PHONE	858-456-5620
EMAIL	info@josephbellows.com
WEB	www.josephbellows.com
STAFF	Joseph Bellows, Mike Mulno, Carol Lee Pryor, Shigeto Miyata
HOURS	Tuesday-Friday, 10-5, and Monday, By Appointment
ARTISTS	Lewis Baltz, Thomas Barrow, Gregory Conniff, Bevan Davies, Betty Hahn, John Humble, David Husom, Charles Johnstone, Elaine Mayes, Philip Melnick, Roger Minick, Grant Mudford, John Pfahl, John Schott, Melissa Shook, Sage Sohier, Wayne Sorce, Jack D. Teemer, Bob Thall, George Tice

Wayne Sorce
Vinegar Hill, Brooklyn, New York, 1985
Digital chromogenic print, 30 × 40 in.

Keith de Lellis Gallery

504

AIPAD Member

Vintage Photography

Photographs by American and European photographers of the 20th century, including vintage Italian photography, fashion, industrial, and New York School.

ADDRESS	41 East 57th Street, Suite 703, New York, NY 10022
PHONE	212-327-1482
EMAIL	keith@keithdelellisgallery.com
WEB	www.keithdelellisgallery.com
STAFF	Keith de Lellis, Nicole Leclair, Peter Fikaris
HOURS	Tuesday-Saturday, 11-5
ARTISTS	Margaret Bourke-White, Louise Dahl-Wolfe, Mario Giacomelli, George Hoyningen-Huene, Simpson Kalisher, Jan Lukas, Nino Migliori, Léonard Misonne, Marvin E. Newman, Edward Quigley, Flip Schulke, Beuford Smith, Anthony Barboza, Edward Steichen, Doris Ulmann, Carl Van Vechten, Weegee, Cecil Beaton, Harold Haliday Costain, Gordon Coster

Flip Schulke
Ali Underwater, 1961
14 × 11 in. & 72 × 48 in.

Kicken Berlin

AIPAD Member

19th-, 20th-, 21st-Century, Vintage, Contemporary, and Modern Photography and Mixed Media

Since 1974, Kicken Gallery has specialized in 19th- and 20th-century and contemporary photography and has explored the medium in more than 220 exhibitions.

ADDRESS Kaiserdamm 118, Berlin, Germany 14057

PHONE +49 30 288 77 88 2

EMAIL kicken@kicken-gallery.com

WEB www.kicken-gallery.com

STAFF Annette Kicken, Petra Helck, Ina Schmidt-Runke

HOURS By Appointment

ARTISTS Bauhaus, Bernd & Hilla Becher, Erwin Blumenfeld, František Drtikol, Jaromír Funke, Rudolf Koppitz, Heinrich Kühn, Helmar Lerski, Man Ray, Werner Mantz, László Moholy-Nagy, Floris M. Neusüss, Albert Renger-Patzsch, Heinrich Riebesehl, Tata Ronkholz, August Sander, Rudolf Schwarzkogler, Otto Steinert, Josef Sudek, Ed van der Elsken

Rudolf Schwarzkogler
3rd Action, 'Untitled', Summer 1965,
Photo: Ludwig Hoffenreich, 1965
Gelatin silver print, printed ca. 1965,
23 × 17.5 cm.
© Estate of Rudolf Schwarzkogler

L. Parker Stephenson Photographs

AIPAD Member

20th-, 21st-Century, Vintage, Contemporary, and Modern Photography

With an interest in overlooked photographers, the Gallery represents US, African,
European and Japanese artists, and curates exhibitions spanning the medium's history.

ADDRESS 764 Madison Avenue, New York, NY 10065

PHONE 212-517-8700

EMAIL info@lparkerstephenson.nyc

WEB www.lparkerstephenson.nyc

STAFF L. Parker Stephenson, Bernard Yenelouis

HOURS Tuesday-Saturday, 11-6

ARTISTS Jane Evelyn Atwood*, Ilse Bing, John Cohen*, John Davies*, Philip Jones
Griffiths, Izis, Kikuji Kawada*, Sirkka-Liisa Konttinen*, Ray Mortenson*,
J.D. 'Okhai Ojeikere, Gilles Peress, Osamu Shiihara, Malick Sidibé,
Jacques Sonck*, Otto Steinert, Paul Strand, Shoji Ueda, UMBO, Witho
Worms*, Jan Yoors*

Artist represented by gallery

Jane Evelyn Atwood
Self-Portrait, New York, 1978
Gelatin silver print
12 × 9.5 in.
© Jane Evelyn Atwood

La Galerie de l'Instant

21st-Century, Vintage, Contemporary, and Modern Photography

La Galerie de l'Instant is a place where all types of photography belong, where everyone is welcome and will find a happy mix of images and styles of photography.

ADDRESS   46 rue de Poitou, Paris, France 75003

PHONE   +33 01 44 54 94 09

EMAIL   julia.gragnon@wanadoo.fr

WEB   www.lagaleriedelinstant.com

STAFF   Julia Gragnon

HOURS   Monday, 2-7, Tuesday-Saturday, 11-7, and Sunday, 2:30-6:30

ARTISTS   Dominique Tarlé, Bert Stern, Bruce Weber, Stephanie Pfriender Stylander, Milton H. Greene, Raymond Cauchetier, Tony Frank, Jean-Pierre Laffont, Terry O'Neill, Ellen Von Unwerth, Paolo Pellegrin, Lucien Clergue, Nicolas Yantchevsky, François Gragnon

Stephanie Pfriender Stylander
Kate Moss, The Face, 1992
Archival digital print, 30 × 45 in.
Edition 5/25
© La Galerie de l'Instant / Stephanie Pfriender Stylander

904 **Laufer**

21st-Century Photography

Laufer is a recognized platform for emerging and established Serbian artists. It showcases Belgrade's most exciting talents, while it helps structure the regional art market.

ADDRESS	Svetozara Radića 4, Belgrade, Serbia 11000
PHONE	+381 66 632 3942
EMAIL	david@laufer.net
WEB	www.lauferart.com
STAFF	Margita Nikolić
HOURS	Daily, 4-8
ARTISTS	Nina Simonović, Vesna Pavlović, Boogie, Dusan Reljin, Sofya Yechina, Dragan Bibin, Boris Lukić, Adrian Klajo

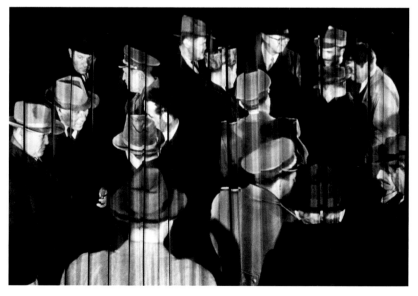

Vesna Pavlović
Fototeka (Projection Still IV), from "Fabrics of Socialism" series, 2015
Archival pigment print on Hahnemühle FineArt Baryta, 50.8 × 76.2 cm.
Edition 2/5
Courtesy of Laufer

LAURENCE MILLER GALLERY

501

AIPAD Member

19th-, 20th-, 21st-Century, Vintage, Contemporary, and Modern Photography and Mixed Media

Laurence Miller Gallery is internationally recognized for its museum quality presentation of both historic and contemporary artwork utilizing photography.

ADDRESS	521 West 26th Street, Fifth Floor, New York, NY 10001
PHONE	212-397-3930
EMAIL	contact@laurencemillergallery.com
WEB	www.laurencemillergallery.com
STAFF	Laurence Miller, Lorraine Koziatek, Jacob Cartwright, Tim Miller
HOURS	Tuesday-Friday, 10-6, and Saturday, 11-6
ARTISTS	Helen Levitt, Ray K. Metzker, Rodrigo Valenzuela, Yoko Ikeda, Toshio Shibata, Simone Rosenbauer, Neal Slavin, Fatemeh Baigmoradi, Fred Herzog, Larry Burrows, Luca Campigotto, Daniel Ranalli, David Graham, Kazuo Sumida, Gary Brotmeyer, Bruce Wrighton, Val Telberg, Denis Darzacq, Harry Callahan

Fatemeh Baigmoradi
From the series "It's Hard to Kill," 2017
Burned photograph, 6 × 8 in.
Unique © Fatemeh Baigmoradi

Lee Gallery

606

AIPAD Member

19th- and 20th-Century Photography

ADDRESS	9 Mount Vernon Street, Winchester, MA 01890
PHONE	781-729-7445
EMAIL	info@leegallery.com
WEB	www.leegallery.com
STAFF	Mack Lee, Michael Lee
HOURS	Monday-Friday, 10-5
ARTISTS	Robert Adams, Eugène Atget, Anna Atkins, Lewis Baltz, Henry P. Bosse, Eugene Cuvelier, Walker Evans, Alexander Gardner, John B. Greene, Gertrude Kasebier, Dorothea Lange, Gustave Le Gray, Charles Nègre, Andrew J. Russell, Edward Steichen, Alfred Stieglitz, Paul Strand, Karl Struss, Carleton Watkins, Edward Weston

Alfred Stieglitz
Equivalent, Series XX, No. 1, 1929
Silver print, 4 5/8 × 3 5/8 in.

Lee Marks Fine Art

AIPAD Member

20th-, 21st-Century, and Contemporary Photography

Established in 1981, LMFA presents bi-monthly, online exhibitions by theme or represented artists. Current and past exhibitions can always be viewed on our website.

ADDRESS	2208 East 350 North, Shelbyville, IN 46176
PHONE	317-696-3324
EMAIL	lee@leemarksfineart.com
WEB	www.leemarksfineart.com
STAFF	Lee Marks, John C. DePrez, Jr.
HOURS	By Appointment
ARTISTS	Gen Aihara, Jeffrey Becom, Andrew Borowiec, Wendy Burton, Mariana Cook, Jen Davis, Lucinda Devlin, Nina Korhonen, Tony Mendoza, Gus Powell, Mike Smith, Martin Usborne

Tony Mendoza
Morning Glories 3, Columbus, Ohio, 2005
Archival inkjet print, 24 × 35 in.
Edition of 20 © Tony Mendoza
Also available: 32 × 45 in., Edition of 5

Lisa Sette Gallery

AIPAD Member

Contemporary Photography and Art

For more than three trailblazing decades, Lisa Sette Gallery has remained committed to discovering and exposing original and intriguing forms of expression.

ADDRESS	210 East Catalina Drive, Phoenix, AZ 85012
PHONE	480-990-7342
EMAIL	sette@lisasettegallery.com
WEB	www.lisasettegallery.com
STAFF	Lisa Sette, Ashley Rice Anderson, Samantha Strom, Melissa Sclafani
HOURS	Tuesday-Friday, 10-5, Saturday, 12-5, and By Appointment
ARTISTS	Damion Berger, Binh Danh, Michael Eastman, Gilbert Garcin, Alan Bur Johnson, Kahn/Selesnick, Mark Klett, Matthew Moore, Marie Navarre, Luis Gonzalez Palma, Luis Molina-Pantin, Fiona Pardington, Charlotte Potter, Mike & Doug Starn, Julianne Swartz, James Turrell, William Wegman

Binh Danh
Spiral Jetty, Utah (#5), 2017
Daguerreotype, 8 × 10 in.
Unique
© Binh Danh

Louise Alexander Gallery

20th-Century, Vintage, and Modern Photography

Established in 2007, Louise Alexander Gallery is a contemporary art gallery based in Porto Cervo, Italy and Los Angeles (2019).

ADDRESS	7083 Hollywood Boulevard, Suite 4085, Los Angeles, CA 90028
PHONE	323-336-7107
EMAIL	info@louise-alexander.com
WEB	www.louise-alexander.com
STAFF	Frederic Arnal, Ayse Arnal
HOURS	Monday-Saturday, 10-7
ARTISTS	Guy Bourdin, Barry X Ball, Enrique Martinez Celaya, Folkert de Jong, Salomon Huerta, Arik Levy, Ryan Mosley, Marco Tirelli

Guy Bourdin
Vogue Paris, 1963
Gelatin silver print, 88.3 × 97.46 cm.
Single edition of 18
© The Guy Bourdin Estate 2019 / Courtesy of Louise Alexander Gallery

MEM, Inc.

AIPAD Member

20th-Century Photography

MEM, Inc. focuses on both contemporary and modern classic photography by Japanese photographers, except for a few European photographers.

ADDRESS	NADiff A/P/A/R/T 3F, 1-18-4 Ebisu, Shibuyaku, Tokyo, Japan 150 0013
PHONE	+81-(0)3-6459-3205
EMAIL	art@mem-inc.jp
WEB	www.mem-inc.jp
STAFF	Katsuya Ishida, Tomoko Ishida, Mizuho Takahashi
HOURS	Daily, 12-8
ARTISTS	Tomoaki Ishihara, Katsumi Omori, Ken Kitano, Ayano Sudo, Antoine d'Agata, Charles Fréger, Keizo Motoda, Yasumasa Morimura, Shigeo Gocho, Iwata Nakayama, Sutezo Otono, Osamu Shiihara, Toru Kono, Gen Otsuka, Yoho Tsuda, Shosuke Sekioka, Shigeru Onishi, Heihachiro Sakai

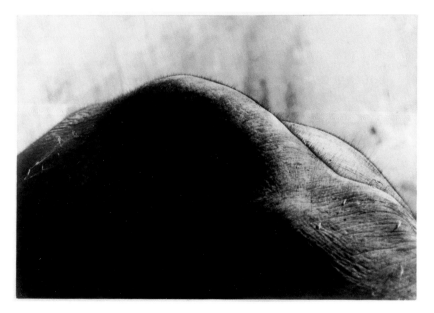

Heihachiro Sakai
Title unknown, c. 1960
Vintage gelatin silver print, 59 × 85.5 cm., Unique
© Naniwa Photography Club, Courtesy of MEM, Inc. Tokyo

603

Michael Hoppen Gallery
AIPAD Member

20th- and 21st-Century Photography

The Michael Hoppen Gallery opened in 1992 and is founded on a passion for photography. We are renowned for nurturing upcoming artists.

ADDRESS	3 Jubilee Place, London, United Kingdom SW3 3TD
PHONE	020 7352 3649
EMAIL	gallery@michaelhoppengallery.com
WEB	www.michaelhoppengallery.com
STAFF	Michael Hoppen, Katy Barron
HOURS	Monday-Friday, 9:30-6, and Saturday, 12-5
ARTISTS	Nobuyoshi Araki, Sian Davey, Eamonn Doyle, Lucas Foglia, Manuel Franquelo, Masahisa Fukase, Juana Gomez, Hiroshi Hamaya, Kati Horna, Eikoh Hosoe, Charles Jones, Thomas Mailaender, Sarah Moon, Sohei Nishino, Gunnar Smoliansky, Shomei Tomatsu, Tim Walker, Harley Weir

Eamonn Doyle
K13, 2018
Archival pigment print, 75 × 56 cm.
Edition of 3
Signed and editioned by the artist

Michael Shapiro Photographs

407 AIPAD Member

20th-Century, Vintage, and Modern Photography

Focus on significant 20th-century, classic, vintage, and black and white photography.

ADDRESS	606 Post Road East, Westport, CT 06880
PHONE	203-222-3899
EMAIL	info@shapirogallery.net
WEB	www.michaelshapirophotographs.com
STAFF	Michael Shapiro
HOURS	By Appointment
ARTISTS	Berenice Abbott, Ansel Adams, Margaret Bourke-White, Ilse Bing, Manuel Álvarez Bravo, Harry Callahan, Henri Cartier-Bresson, Imogen Cunningham, Walker Evans, Consuelo Kanaga, André Kertész, Alma Lavenson, Irving Penn, Frederick Sommer, Josef Sudek, Willard Van Dyke, Brett Weston, Edward Weston, Max Dupain

Max Dupain
Sunbaker, Negative: 1937 (printed later)
Gelatin silver print, 13 1/4 × 16 1/2 in. (image size)
© Estate of Max Dupain

901 Momentum Fine Art

Contemporary and Modern Photography

Momentum Fine Art is a fine art photography gallery and art consultant based in Miami, Florida. Momentum Fine Art represents mid-career and emerging fine art photography.

ADDRESS	6014 SW 22nd Street, Miami, FL 33155
PHONE	305-799-6960
EMAIL	info@momentumfineart.com
WEB	www.momentumfineart.com
STAFF	Vincent Milner, Devika Milner, Aristotle Roufanis, Ole Marius Joergensen
HOURS	By Appointment
ARTISTS	Aristotle Roufanis, Ole Marius Joergensen, BJ & Richelle Formento, Maria Svarbova, Jacob Howard, Javiera Estrada, Christophe Jarcot, Fang Tong, Cristina Coral, Ian Patrick O'Connor

Aristotle Roufanis
Alone Together VIII, 2017
Pigment print on Fine Art Baryta paper, 57 1/10 × 66 9/10 in.
Edition of 5 + 2 Artist Proofs © Aristotle Roufanis

Monroe Gallery of Photography
AIPAD Member

20th-, 21st-Century, Vintage, and Contemporary Photography

Building on more than five decades of collective experience, the Gallery emphasizes 20th- and 21st-century photojournalism.

ADDRESS	112 Don Gaspar Avenue, Santa Fe, NM, 87501
PHONE	505-992-0800
EMAIL	info@monroegallery.com
WEB	www.monroegallery.com
STAFF	Sidney Monroe, Michelle Monroe
HOURS	Daily, 10-5
ARTISTS	Eddie Adams, Nina Berman, Whitney Curtis, John Dominis, Alfred Eisenstaedt, Bill Eppridge, Ernst Haas, Ashley Gilbertson, Bob Gomel, Joe McNally, Carl Mydans, Bill Ray, Steve Schapiro, Art Shay, Tony Vaccaro, Grey Villet, Ryan Vizzions, Stephen Wilkes

Tony Vaccaro
Newly liberated women in Nante, along the North bank of the Loire River, celebrate their freedom, Nante, France, July, 1944
Archival pigment print, 11 × 14 in.
Edition of 15 © Tony Vaccaro

803

only photography

AIPAD Member

20th- 21st-Century, Vintage, and Contemporary Photography

Gallery and publishing house for classic and contemporary photography, focus on Japanese and European photography of the '60s/'70s. High quality photo books in limited editions.

ADDRESS   Niebuhrstrasse 78, Berlin, Germany 10629

PHONE   +49-30-847 20 291

EMAIL   info@only-photography.com

WEB   www.only-photography.com

STAFF   Roland Angst, Minami Shimagake

HOURS   Wednesday-Friday, 2-7, and Saturday, 12-5

ARTISTS   Stéphane Duroy, Frauke Eigen, Marina Faust, Gerry Johansson, Peter Keetman, Osamu Kanemura, Kazuo Kitai, Viktor Kolar, Ray K. Metzker, Kosuke Okahara, Toni Schneiders, Wilhelm Schürmann, Toshio Shibata, Gunnar Smoliansky, Joseph Sterling, Issei Suda, Yutaka Takanashi, Shomei Tomatsu, Bruce Wrighton, Shin Yanagisawa

Issei Suda
Yokohama Sankeien Garden, Kanagawa, 1977
Gelatin silver print, 168 × 172 mm.
© Issei Suda
From the series: Sushi Kaden

Pace/MacGill Gallery

AIPAD Member

Contemporary, Modern, and Vintage Photography

Pace/MacGill Gallery was founded in 1983 by Peter MacGill, in collaboration with partners Arne Glimcher of Pace Gallery and Richard Solomon of Pace Prints and Pace African and Oceanic Art.

ADDRESS	32 East 57th Street, Ninth Floor, New York, NY 10022
PHONE	212-759-7999
EMAIL	info@pacemacgill.com
WEB	www.pacemacgill.com
STAFF	Peter MacGill, Kimberly Jones, Lauren Panzo, Margaret Kelly, Kaelan Kleber
HOURS	Tuesday–Saturday, 10-6
ARTISTS	Richard Avedon, Yto Barrada, Harry Callahan, William Christenberry, Robert Frank, Jim Goldberg, David Goldblatt, Emmet Gowin, Paul Graham, Peter Hujar, Josef Koudelka, Richard Learoyd, Richard Misrach, Yoshitomo Nara, Irving Penn, Paolo Roversi, Michal Rovner, Fazal Sheikh, Kiki Smith, JoAnn Verburg

Richard Learoyd
French Tulips with Cotton Grid, 2018
Camera obscura Ilfochrome
photograph mounted to aluminum
32 × 25 in.
One of three unique variants
© Richard Learoyd/Courtesy of Pace
and Pace/MacGill, New York

Paul M. Hertzmann, Inc.

AIPAD Member

19th- & 20th-Century Vintage Photography

American & European Modernism, Photo-Secession, f/64, post World War II, the American West.

ADDRESS	PO Box 40447, San Francisco, CA 94140
PHONE	415-626-2677
EMAIL	pmhi@hertzmann.net
WEB	www.hertzmann.net
STAFF	Paul Hertzmann, Susan Herzig
HOURS	By Appointment
ARTISTS	Ansel Adams, Eugéne Atget, Bill Brandt, Brassaï, Imogen Cunningham, Ei-Q, T. Lux Feininger, Gerard Fieret, Dorothea Lange, Tina Modotti, Moholy-Nagy, Arnulf Rainer, Man Ray, Marcia Resnick, Aaron Siskind, Alfred Stieglitz, Paul Strand, Carleton Watkins, Edward Weston, Minor White

Edward Weston
Dunes, Oceano, 1936
Vintage silver print, 7 1/8 × 9 5/8 in.
© The Center for Creative Photography, University of Arizona, Tucson, AZ

604

PDNB Gallery

AIPAD Member

20th-Century and Contemporary Photography and Mixed Media

Established in Dallas, Texas in 1995. Exhibiting local, national, and international artists.

ADDRESS	154 Glass Street, Suite 104, Dallas, TX 75207
PHONE	214-969-1852
EMAIL	info@pdnbgallery.com
WEB	www.pdnbgallery.com
STAFF	Missy S. Finger, Burt Finger, Luisa Goldstein, Meredith Rendell
HOURS	Tuesday-Saturday, 11-5
ARTISTS	John Albok, Jesse Alexander, Lucienne Bloch, Peter Brown, Keith Carter, Carlotta Corpron, Jack Delano, Esteban Pastorino Diaz, Morris Engel, Elliott Erwitt, Earlie Hudnall, Michael Kenna, Ida Lansky, Chema Madoz, Cheryl Medow, Jeanine Michna-Bales, Delilah Montoya, Nickolas Muray, Bill Owens, Jeffrey Silverthorne

Cheryl Medow
White Ibis with Fish, 2014
Archival pigment print
© Cheryl Medow, Courtesy of PDNB Gallery

Peter Fetterman Gallery

AIPAD Member

20th-, 21st-Century, and Modern Photography

Peter Fetterman Gallery has one of the largest inventories of classic 20th-century photography in the country, particularly in humanist photography.

ADDRESS	2525 Michigan Avenue, Santa Monica, CA 90404
PHONE	310-453-6463
EMAIL	info@peterfetterman.com
WEB	www.peterfetterman.com
STAFF	Peter Fetterman, Ryan McIntosh, Michael Hulett, David Jones
HOURS	Wednesday-Saturday, 11-6
ARTISTS	Sebastião Salgado, Sarah Moon, Jeffrey Conley, Richard Corman, Noell Oszvald, Ernesto Esquer, David Montgomery

Sebastião Salgado
Suruwaha, Amazonas, Brazil, 2017
Gelatin silver print, 24 × 35 in.
© Amazonas Images/Courtesy of Peter Fetterman Gallery

PGI

608

AIPAD Member

20th-Century and Contemporary Photography

PGI has introduced selected photographers and worked with Japanese masters representing post-war photography. We also take pride in partnership with up-and-coming artists.

ADDRESS   TKB bldg. 3F, 2-3-4 Higashi Azabu, Minatoku, Tokyo, Japan 106-0044

PHONE   +81 3-5114-7935

EMAIL   info-e@pgi.ac

WEB   www.pgi.ac/en

STAFF   Masayuki Nishimaru, Shigeko Nozaki, Sayaka Takahashi, Takayuki Ogawa, Mie Akiyama, Yoshihisa Yoshida

HOURS   Monday-Friday, 11-7, and Saturday, 11-6

ARTISTS   Takashi Arai, Yuji Hamada, Naohisa Hara, Yasuhiro Ishimoto, Yoshihiko Ito, Kikuji Kawada, Michiko Kon, Yasunori Marui, Kozo Miyoshi, O. James Nakagawa, Ikko Narahara, Mitsugu Ohnishi, SATO Shintaro, Tomio Seike, Kazuyuki Soeno, Issei Suda, Munemasa Takahashi, Hiroyuki Takenouchi, Tokuko Ushioda, Kiyoshi Yagi

Tokuko Ushioda
Bibliotheca, #3,
Gelatin silver print,
13 × 13 in.
Edition of 5
© Tokuko Ushioda /
Courtesy of PGI

Polka Galerie

21st-Century, Vintage, and Contemporary Photography

Founded in 2007 by sister and brother Adélie de Ipanema and Edouard Genestar, Polka Galerie is located in Paris's Marais area.

ADDRESS	Cour de Venise, 12 rue Saint Gilles, Paris, France 75003
PHONE	+33 1 76 21 41 31
EMAIL	contact@polkagalerie.com
WEB	www.polkagalerie.com
STAFF	Adélie de Ipanema, Sidonie Gaychet
HOURS	Tuesday-Saturday, 11-7
ARTISTS	Jacob Aue Sobol, Nicolas Comment, Richard Dumas, Elliott Erwitt, Joakim Eskildsen, Mario Giacomelli, Alexander Gronsky, Matt Henry, William Klein, Jacques Henri Lartigue, Lek Sowat, Sze Tsung Nicolas Leong, Yves Marchand & Romain Meffre, Joel Meyerowitz, Claude Nori, Kosuke Okahara, Jean Marie Périer, Marc Riboud, Sebastião Salgado, Toshio Shibata

Yves Marchand & Romain Meffre
Paramount theater, Brooklyn, USA, 2018
Cibachrome print, 100 × 150 cm.
Edition of 3 © Yves Marchand & Romain Meffre

704

Richard Moore Photographs
AIPAD Member

Vintage Photographs from the 19th and 20th Centuries

Private dealer of photographs since 2000. Specialties include the Photo-Secession, Group f/64, FSA photographers, social documentary work, and California photography.

ADDRESS PO Box 16245, Oakland, CA 94610

PHONE 510-271-0149

EMAIL info@richardmoorephoto.com

WEB www.richardmoorephoto.com

STAFF Richard Moore

HOURS By Appointment

ARTISTS Berenice Abbott, Ansel Adams, Anne Brigman, Imogen Cunningham, Walker Evan, David Goldblatt, Dorothea Lange, Russell Lee, Helen Levitt, Margrethe Mather, Richard Misrach, Tina Modotti, Eadweard Muybridge, Peter Sekaer, Ben Shahn, Frederick Sommer, Karl Struss, Weegee, Edward Weston, Max Yavno

Dorothea Lange
Martin Pulich, Public Defender, 1957
Vintage gelatin silver print, 10 9/16 × 13 in.
© The Dorothea Lange Collection, Oakland Museum of California

Robert Klein Gallery

AIPAD Member

19th-, 20th-, 21st-Century, Vintage, Contemporary, and Modern Photography and Mixed Media

Established in 1980.

ADDRESS	38 Newbury Street, Boston, MA 02116
PHONE	617-267-7997
EMAIL	inquiry@robertkleingallery.com
WEB	www.robertkleingallery.com
STAFF	Hank Hauptmann, Robert Klein
HOURS	Tuesday-Friday, 10-5:30, Saturday, 11-5, and By Appointment
ARTISTS	Julie Blackmon, Gohar Dashti, Sally Gall, Cig Harvey, Bill Jacobson, Yousuf Karsh, György Kepes, Helen Levitt, Man Ray, Constantine Manos, Rania Matar, Olivia Parker, Gordon Parks, Sebastião Salgado, Rodney Smith, Paulette Tavormina, Alex Webb, Edward Weston, Stephen Wilkes, Francesca Woodman

Rania Matar
Wafaa and Sanaa, Bourj El Barajneh Refugee Camp, Beirut, Lebanon, 2017
Archival digital pigment print, 28.8 × 36 in.
Edition of 6 © Rania Matar

Robert Koch Gallery

AIPAD Member

19th-Century, 20th-Century, and Contemporary Photography
Established in 1979.

ADDRESS	49 Geary Street, 5th Floor, San Francisco, CA 94108
PHONE	415-421-0122
EMAIL	info@kochgallery.com
WEB	www.kochgallery.com
STAFF	Robert Koch, Ada Takahashi, David Carmona
HOURS	Tuesday-Saturday, 10:30-5:30
ARTISTS	Ljubodrag Andric, Edward Burtynsky, Tamas Dezso, Chris Dorley-Brown, František Drtikol, Elliott Erwitt, Jaromír Funke, Adam Katseff, György Kepes, André Kertész, Josef Koudelka, Karine Laval, Gustave Le Gray, Man Ray, László Moholy-Nagy, Mimi Plumb, Josef Sudek, Carleton E. Watkins and Alex Webb, Rebecca Norris Webb, Michael Wolf

Josef Ehm
Neons, c. 1930s
Vintage gelatin silver print
4 5/8 × 3 3/8 in.

502

Robert Mann Gallery
AIPAD Member

20th-, 21st-Century, Vintage, Contemporary, and Modern Photography
Founded in 1985, Robert Mann Gallery specializes in 20th-century masters of photography and represents an international roster contemporary artists working in photo-based art.

ADDRESS	525 West 26th Street, Second Floor, New York, NY 10001
PHONE	212-989-7600
EMAIL	mail@robertmann.com
WEB	www.robertmann.com
STAFF	Robert Mann, Caroline Wall, Madeline Cornell, Emma Ressel
HOURS	Tuesday-Friday, 10-6, and Saturday, 11-6
ARTISTS	Ansel Adams, Holly Andres, Ellen Auerbach, Julie Blackmon, Jeff Brouws, Joe Deal, Richard Finkelstein, Murray Fredericks, Elijah Gowin, Cig Harvey, Elisabeth Hase, Chip Hooper, Michael Kenna, Maroesjka Lavigne, Herman Leonard, Mike Mandel, Ed Sievers, Aaron Siskind, Paulette Tavormina, Margaret Watkins

Cig Harvey
Jesse in the Fog, Pink Coat, 2018
Chromogenic dye coupler print
40 × 30 in.
Edition of 7 © Cig Harvey, Courtesy of Robert Mann Gallery, New York

109 RocioSantaCruz

Vintage and Contemporary Photography and Mixed Media

RocioSantaCruz Gallery is a dynamic space devoted to contemporary art, photography, experimental cinema, and the archive and publication of artists' books.

ADDRESS Gran Via de les Corts Catalanes 627, Barcelona, Spain 08010

PHONE +34 936 338 360

EMAIL info@rociosantacruz.com

WEB www.rociosantacruz.com

STAFF Rocio Santa Cruz, Isabel Sozzi

HOURS Tuesday-Friday, 10-2 and 4-8, Saturday, 12-8

ARTISTS Mar Arza, Blanca Casas Brullet, Jean Denant, Pep Duran, Gonzalo Elvira, Andrés Galeano, Ferran Garcia Sevilla, Ana Garcia-Pineda, Marcel Giró, Lluís Hortalà, Julia Llerena, German Lorca, Oriol Maspons, Marina Núñez, Lois Patiño, Palmira Puig-Giró, Rubens Teixeira Scavone, Montserrat Soto, Miguel Trillo, Sergio Vega

Palmira Puig-Giró
Sem Título, 1950
Vintage silver gelatin on paper
40 × 30 cm.
Unique
© Palmira Puig-Giró, Courtesy of
RocioSantaCruz

Rolf Art

AIPAD Member

21st-Century, Vintage, and Contemporary Latin American Photography

Rolf Art focuses on contemporary Latin American visual arts. The gallery features works exploring photographic media and its boundaries.

ADDRESS   Esmeralda 1353, Buenos Aires, Argentina 1007ABS

PHONE   +54 11 4326-3679

EMAIL   info@rolfart.com.ar

WEB   www.rolfart.com.ar

STAFF   Florencia Giordana, Camila Knowles, Julieta Tarraubella

HOURS   Monday-Friday, 11-8

ARTISTS   Ananké Asseff, Marcelo Brodsky, Facundo de Zuviría, Adriana Lestido, Milagros de la Torre, Roberto Huarcaya, Marcos López, Liliana Maresca, Santiago Porter, Graciela Sacco, Gabriel Valansi, Humberto Rivas, Silvia Rivas, Francisco Medail, Vivian Galban, Jackie Parisier, RES Stolkiner, Jackie Parisier

Humberto Rivas
From the portraits series, Luci, 1990
Polyptych composed of 9 gelatin silver prints on fiber paper, 40 × 40 cm. each
© Humberto Rivas Courtesy of Rolf Art Gallery

Scheinbaum & Russek, Ltd.

AIPAD Member

20th-Century, Vintage, Contemporary, and Modern Photography

Established in 1980, Scheinbaum & Russek, Ltd. possess a rare combination of expertise as gallerists, educators, and photographers. Certified member of the Appraisers Association of America.

ADDRESS	369 Montezuma #345, Santa Fe, NM 87501
PHONE	505-988-5116
EMAIL	srltd@photographydealers.com
WEB	www.photographydealers.com
STAFF	Janet Russek, David Scheinbaum, Andra Russek
HOURS	By Appointment
ARTISTS	Ansel Adams, Manuel Álvarez Bravo, Harry Callahan, Paul Caponigro, Manuel Carrillo, Henri Cartier-Bresson, Lynn Geesaman, Laura Gilpin, Luis González Palma, Estate of Beaumont Newhall, Estate of Nancy Newhall, Olivia Parker, Estate of Eliot Porter, Sebastião Salgado, Aaron Siskind, Ralph Steiner, Alfred Stieglitz, Jerry Uelsmann, Edward Weston, Minor White

Eliot Porter (1901 - 1990)
Parula Warbler, Parula Americana, Great Spruce Head Island, 1968
Dye-transfer print, 8 1/2 × 10 in. (Mount 20 × 24 in.)
© 1990, Amon Carter Museum, Fort Worth, Texas, Bequest of Eliot Porter

Scott Nichols Gallery

AIPAD Member

19th-, 20th-, 21st-Century, and Vintage Photography

A private dealer since 1980, Scott Nichols opened the gallery in 1992, specializing in classic and contemporary photography with an emphasis on Group f/64.

ADDRESS	49 Geary Street, Suite 415, San Francisco, CA 94108
PHONE	415-788-4641
EMAIL	info@scottnicholsgallery.com
WEB	www.scottnicholsgallery.com
STAFF	Scott Nichols, Ann Jastrab
HOURS	Tuesday-Friday, 11-5:30, and Saturday, 11-5
ARTISTS	Ansel Adams, Ruth Bernhard, Anne Brigman, Horace Bristol, Wynn Bullock, Paul Caponigro, Imogen Cunningham, Edward S. Curtis, Judy Dater, William Garnett, Mona Kuhn, Dorothea Lange, Danny Lyon, Barbara Morgan, Irving Penn, W. Eugene Smith, Paul Strand, George Tice, Brett Weston, Edward Weston

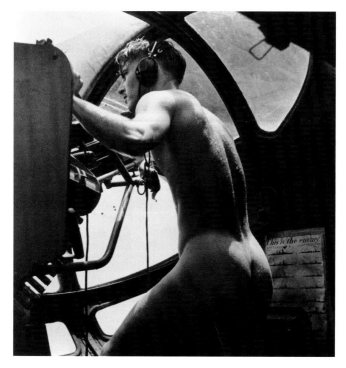

Horace Bristol
PBY Blister Gunner,
Rescue at Rabaul,
1944
Gelatin silver print
17 1/2 × 17 1/2 in.

Sears-Peyton Gallery

Contemporary Photography.

Contemporary American art gallery in Chelsea, New York City with a private viewing space in Brentwood, Los Angeles.

ADDRESS	210 11th Avenue, Suite 802, New York, NY 10001
PHONE	212-966-7469
EMAIL	info@searspeyton.com
WEB	www.searspeyton.com
STAFF	Gaines Peyton, Macie Sears, Sarah Moore, Bryan Rogers
HOURS	Monday-Friday, 10-6, and Saturday, 11-6
ARTISTS	Agnes Barley, Isabel Bigelow, Poogy Bjerklie, Maysey Craddock, Celia Gerard, Tyler Haughey, John Huggins, Patricia Iglesias, Bo Joseph, Kathryn Lynch, Jane Rosen, Lourdes Sanchez, Rick Shaefer, Wendy Small, Suzy Spence, MaryBeth Thielhelm, Cecil Touchon, Jen Wink Hays, Jason Frank Rothenberg, Andrew Zimmerman

Tyler Haughey
Gold Crest Resort Motel, 2016
Archival pigment print, 56 × 70 in.
Edition of 5 © Tyler Haughey

Sous Les Etoiles Gallery

305

AIPAD Member

21st-Century Photography

Sous Les Etoiles Gallery is a contemporary exhibition space specializing in fine art photography and photo-based art.

ADDRESS	100 Crosby Street, #603, New York, NY 10012
PHONE	212-966-0796
EMAIL	info@souslesetoilesgallery.net
WEB	www.souslesetoilesgallery.net
STAFF	Corinne Tapia, Sylvere Azoulai, Dawn Goodrich
HOURS	Monday-Saturday, 12-6
ARTISTS	Ernesto Bazan, Carolle Benitah, Julie Boserup, Richard Caldicott, Gianfranco Chiavacci Estate, Robin Cracknell, Luuk de Haan, James Whitlow Delano, Sophie Delaporte, Andreas Gefeller, Eeva Hannula, Gottfried Jager, Alberto Korda Estate, Jean-Pierre Laffont, Charles Petillon, Georges Rousse, Javier Riera, Barry Underwood, Susann Wellm, David Zimmerman

Marleen Sleeuwits
Interior #53, 2019
Ultrachrome print, Edition of 5
© Marleen Sleeuwits
Courtesy of Sous Les Etoiles Gallery

Staley-Wise Gallery
AIPAD Member

20th-, 21st-Century, Vintage, Contemporary, Modern, and Fashion Photography

Founded in 1981. Staley-Wise Gallery focuses on fashion photography and presents excellence in the genre by master photographers, influencing the greater art world.

ADDRESS	100 Crosby Street, Suite 305, New York, NY 10012
PHONE	212-966-6223
EMAIL	photo@staleywise.com
WEB	www.staleywise.com
STAFF	Etheleen Staley, Taki Wise, George Kocis
HOURS	Tuesday-Saturday, 11-5
ARTISTS	Slim Aarons, Richard Avedon, Lillian Bassman, Harry Benson, Louise Dahl-Wolfe, Micheal Dweck, Arthur Elgort, William Helburn, Horst P. Horst, Daniel Kramer, David LaChapelle, Kurt Markus, Sheila Metzner, Genevieve Naylor, Helmut Newton, Herb Ritts, Melvin Sokolsky, Bert Stern, Deborah Turbeville, Ellen Von Unwerth

David LaChapelle
Elizabeth Taylor: National Velvet, Burbank, 2002
Archival pigment print, 30 × 40 in.
Edition of 5
© David LaChapelle

Stephen Bulger Gallery

AIPAD Member

19th-, 20th-, 21st-Century, Vintage, Contemporary, and Modern Photography

Since 1995, the gallery has sustained an active exhibition schedule of both historical and contemporary photographers from across Canada and around the world.

ADDRESS   1356 Dundas Street West, Toronto, ON, Canada M6J 1Y2

PHONE   416-504-0575

EMAIL   info@bulgergallery.com

WEB   www.bulgergallery.com

STAFF   Stephen Bulger, Sarah Burtscher, Robyn Zolnai, Jennifer Lindsay, Scott Poborsa, Sasha Furlani

HOURS   Tuesday-Saturday, 11-6

ARTISTS   Sara Angelucci, Phil Bergerson, Robert Burley, Scott Conarroe, Lutz Dille, Charles Gagnon, Gilbert Garcin, Richard Harrington, Dave Heath, Clive Holden, Sarah Anne Johnson, Gábor Kerekes, André Kertész, Rita Leistner, Meryl McMaster, Sanaz Mazinani, Louie Palu, Deanna Pizzitelli, Alison Rossiter, Larry Towell

Meryl McMaster
From a Still Unquiet Place, 2019
Chromogenic print, 40 × 60 in.
© Meryl McMaster

Stephen Daiter Gallery

AIPAD Member

701

20th-, 21st-Century, Vintage, and Contemporary Photography

Stephen Daiter Gallery offers fine contemporary and vintage examples of important American and European photography from the 20th and 21st centuries.

ADDRESS	230 West Superior Street, Fourth Floor, Chicago, IL 60654
PHONE	312-787-3350
EMAIL	info@stephendaitergallery.com
WEB	www.stephendaitergallery.com
STAFF	Stephen Daiter, Lucas Zenk, Allison Parssi, Dan Mrotek
HOURS	Wednesday-Saturday, 11-5
ARTISTS	Dawoud Bey, Lynne Cohen, Barbara Crane, Paul D'Amato, Elliott Erwitt, John Gossage, Kenneth Josephson, André Kertész, Susan Meiselas, Wayne Miller, Marvin Newman, Martin Parr, Eugene Richards, Gary Schneider, Joseph Sterling, Charles Swedlund, Alex Webb, Sabine Weiss, Gyorgy Kepes, Aaron Siskind

Dawoud Bey
Untitled #12 (The Marsh), 2017
Gelatin silver photograph, 48 × 59 in.
Edition of 6 © Dawoud Bey

Throckmorton Fine Art, Inc.

AIPAD Member

19th-, 20th-, 21st-Century, Vintage, Contemporary, and Modern Photography and Mixed Media

Throckmorton Fine Art, Inc. is a New York-based gallery that specializes in Latin American vintage and contemporary photography.

ADDRESS   145 East 57th Street, Third Floor, New York, NY 10022

PHONE   212-223-1059

EMAIL   info@throckmorton-nyc.com

WEB   www.throckmorton-nyc.com

STAFF   Spencer S. Throckmorton, Norberto L. Rivera, Dimitri Treantafilos

HOURS   Tuesday-Saturday, 10-5

ARTISTS   Ruven Afanador, Flor Garduño, Mario Algaze, Graciela Iturbide, Henri Cartier-Bresson, Manuel Álvarez Bravo, Lola Álvarez Bravo, Marilyn Bridges, Lucien Clergue, Valdir Cruz, Lynn Gilbert, George Platt Lynes, Tina Modotti, Héctor García, Nickolas Muray, Fritz Henle, Mario Cravo Neto, Dimitris Yeros, Mariana Yampolsky, Edward Weston

Manuel Álvarez Bravo
The Good Reputation Sleeping / La buena fama durmiendo, 1939
Platinum palladium print, 7 × 9 in.
© 2018, Estate of Manuel Álvarez Bravo

Todd Webb Archive

20th-Century and Vintage Photography

The Todd Webb Archive was established to educate the public about 20th-century photographer Todd Webb. This year, the archive is making rare, never-before-seen vintage work available.

ADDRESS	61 Pleasant Street, Portland, ME 04101
PHONE	207-879-0042
EMAIL	info@toddwebbarchive.com
WEB	www.toddwebbarchive.com
STAFF	Betsy Evans Hunt, Sam Walker, Chris Hunt, Rose Marasco
HOURS	By Appointment
ARTISTS	Todd Webb

Todd Webb
Mr. Perkins Pierce Arrow, New York, 1946
Gelatin silver print, 11 × 14 in.
© Todd Webb Archive, Portland, Maine, USA

Toluca Fine Art

Latin American Photography

Toluca mainly champions artists from Latin America, many of whom have been the subject in recent years of exhibitions curated by Alexis Fabry, director of the gallery.

ADDRESS	38 rue des Blancs Manteaux, Paris, France 75004
PHONE	+33 1 42 72 65 76
EMAIL	alexistoluca@wanadoo.fr
WEB	www.tolucafineart.com
STAFF	Alexis Fabry, Laurent Bosque
HOURS	Monday-Friday, 10-7
ARTISTS	Enrique Bostelmann, Alfredo Boulton, Johanna Calle, Armando Cristeto, Milagros de la Torre, Facundo de Zuviría, Paz Errázuriz, Fernell Franco, Paolo Gasparini, Pablo Hare, Jorge Heredia, Graciela Iturbide, Pablo López Luz, Enrique Metinides, Pablo Ortíz Monasterio, Oscar Pintor, Miguel Rio Branco, Victor Robledo, Miguel Ángel Rojas, Juan Travnik

Facundo de Zuviría
Lavadero en Manantiales, Uruguay, 1991-2019
Dye transfer print, 30 × 40 cm.
Limited edition of 5 © Facundo de Zuviria

UNIX Gallery

21st-Century and Contemporary Photography

Founded as a secondary market gallery in London, UNIX Gallery remains dedicated to presenting thought provoking, immersive exhibitions that engender a strong artistic impact.

ADDRESS 507 West 27th Street, New York, NY 10001

PHONE 212-209-1572

EMAIL info@unixgallery.com

WEB www.unixgallery.com

STAFF Alex Cesaria, Daniela Mercuri, Andrew Cole

HOURS Tuesday-Saturday, 10-6

ARTISTS Peter Anton, Justin Bower, William Bradley, Jonathan Paul, Ellen de Meijer, Pablo Dona, Richard Garet, Marcello Lo Giudice, Eugenio Merino, John Messinger, C. Michael Norton, Josh Rowell, KwangHo Shin, Christian Voigt, Llewellyn Xavier

Christian Voigt
Tyrannosaurus Rex, 2018
LiteJet exposure on Alu-dibond behind museum glass, 84 × 61 in. (213 × 155 cm.)
Edition of 12 © UNIX Gallery

Utópica
AIPAD Member

Vintage, Modern, and Contemporary Brazilian Photography

Founded in 2007, Utópica is dedicated to appreciating collections of the early 20th-century photographers. Utópica encourages and guides current work by young photographers.

ADDRESS   Rua Rodésia 26, São Paulo, Brazil 05435020

PHONE   (55-11) 3037-7349

EMAIL   info@utopica.photography

WEB   www.utopica.photography

STAFF   Pablo Di Giulio, Marcella Brandimarti, Diógenes Moura, Paula Viecelli

HOURS   Tuesday-Friday, 11-7, and Saturday, 11-5

ARTISTS   German Lorca, José Yalenti, Foto Cine Clube Bandeirante, Carlos Moreira, Luiz Carlos Felizardo, André Cunha Felipe Russo, Evandro Teixeira, Wagner Almeida

German Lorca
*Self-portrait in
downtown São Paulo,* 1957
Unique vintage gelatin silver print
14 3/4 × 11 1/8 in.
© German Lorca/Courtesy of Utópica,
São Paulo

902 Voltz Clarke Gallery

Contemporary

Voltz Clarke Gallery is a New York contemporary art gallery representing emerging and mid-career artists.

ADDRESS	141 East 62nd St, Second Floor, New York, NY 10065
PHONE	212-933-0291
EMAIL	info@voltzclarke.com
WEB	www.voltzclarke.com
STAFF	Blair Clarke, Sarah Tortorich, Alistair Clarke, Caroline Joseph
HOURS	Monday-Friday, 10-6, and Saturday, By Appointment
ARTISTS	Natasha Law, Bradley Sabin, Heather Chontos, Landon Nordeman, Jacinto Moros, Nancy Richardson, Sara Genn, Sasha Sykes, Gemma Gené, Lisa Shulte, Joshua Avery Webster, Stephanie Patton, Jeff Chester, Lucy Soni, Katy Ferrarone, Christina Burch, Yiorgos Kordakis, Holland Cunningham

Nancy Richardson
Soho Site II, 2013-18
Archival pigment print, 88 × 84 in.
Edition of 7

Wach Gallery

AIPAD Member

Vintage and Contemporary Photography

Fine vintage and contemporary photographs.

ADDRESS	31860 Walker Road, Avon Lake, OH 44012
PHONE	440-933-2780
EMAIL	mail@wachgallery.com
WEB	www.wachgallery.com
STAFF	Peter M. Wach, Judith Wach
HOURS	By Appointment
ARTISTS	Berenice Abbott, Ansel Adams, Ruth Bernhard, Brassaï, Margaret Bourke-White, Robert Doisneau, David H. Gibson, Walter Grossman, Philippe Halsman, Carl Austin Hyatt, Yousuf Karsh, Robert Glenn Ketchum, André Kertész, Barbara Morgan, Edward Steichen, Alfred Stieglitz, Paul Strand, Brett Weston, Edward Weston, Minor White

Barbara Morgan
American Document, 1940 "We Are Three Women - We Are Three Million Women"
Gelatin silver, 11 × 14 in.
© Barbara Morgan

Weinstein Hammons Gallery

AIPAD Member

Contemporary and Modern Photography

Since 1996, Weinstein Hammons Gallery has worked with internationally recognized artists working in all media, with a special focus on modern and contemporary photography.

ADDRESS	908 West 46th Street, Minneapolis, MN 55419
PHONE	612-822-1722
EMAIL	info@weinsteinhammons.com
WEB	www.weinsteinhammons.com
STAFF	Martin Weinstein, Leslie Hammons, Benjamin Reed
HOURS	Tuesday–Saturday, 12-5, and By Appointment
ARTISTS	Cass Bird, Edward Burtynsky, Elliott Erwitt, Annie Leibovitz, Vera Lutter, Erik Madigan Heck, Robert Mapplethorpe, Magnus Nilsson, Gordon Parks, Nancy Rexroth, Alec Soth, Paolo Ventura

Alec Soth
Dan-George, Dusseldorf, 2018
Archival pigment print, 40 × 32 in.
Edition of 9
© Weinstein Hammons Gallery

503

William L. Schaeffer Photographic Works of Art
AIPAD Member

19th-, 20th-Century, Vintage, and Classic Press Photography
19th- and 20th-century and vintage photographs. Since 1974, we have dealt with an exceptional range of photographic works of art, including daguerreotypes and press images.

ADDRESS	PO Box 296, Chester, CT 06412
PHONE	860-526-3870
EMAIL	wmls@me.com
WEB	www.williamlschaeffer.com
STAFF	Skip Weisenburger
HOURS	Monday-Friday, 9-5, and By Appointment
ARTISTS	Ansel Adams, William Bell, Margaret Bourke-White, Adolphe Braun, Manuel Álvarez Bravo, Eugène Cuvelier, Bruce Davidson, Walker Evans, Roger Fenton, John Moran, Timothy O'Sullivan, David Plowden, Andrew J. Russell, W. Eugene Smith, William J. Stillman, Isaiah W. Taber, Carleton E. Watkins, Weegee, Edward Weston, Minor White

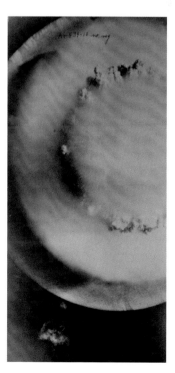

Unknown
Nuclear Test Explosion, Bikini Atoll, c. 1946
Gelatin silver print, 17 3/4 × 8 3/4 in.

Winter Works on Paper

AIPAD Member

19th-, 20th-Century, Vintage, and Photography and Photojournalism

We get the ones that got away.

ADDRESS	167 North Ninth Street, Apartment 11, Brooklyn, NY 11211
PHONE	718-599-0910
EMAIL	winterworks@verizon.net
WEB	www.winterworksonpaper.com
STAFF	David Winter
HOURS	By Appointment
ARTISTS	Unknown, Weegee, Lee Friedlander, Walker Evans, John Gutmann, Alfred Eisenstaedt

Salomon Nadelman
Mississippi Baptism, 1961
Gelatin silver print, 8 × 10 in.

Yancey Richardson Gallery
AIPAD Member

20th-, 21st-Century, and Contemporary Photography

Founded in 1995, Yancey Richardson is one of the preeminent galleries of photo-based art.

ADDRESS	525 West 22nd Street, New York, NY 10011
PHONE	646-230-9610
EMAIL	info@yanceyrichardson.com
WEB	www.yanceyrichardson.com
STAFF	Matthew Whitworth, Sarah Cope, Alex Pigeon, Nicholas Hall
HOURS	Tuesday-Saturday, 10-6
ARTISTS	Olivo Barbieri, Jared Bark, Mary Ellen Bartley, Sharon Core, Mitch Epstein, Ori Gersht, Bryan Graf, Anthony Hernandez, Lisa Kereszi, Laura Letinsky, Andrew Moore, Zanele Muholi, Rachel Perry, Sebastião Salgado, Victoria Sambunaris, Mark Steinmetz, Larry Sultan, Mickalene Thomas, Hellen van Meene, Masao Yamamoto

Larry Sultan
Woman in Curlers, 2002
Archival pigment print, 50 × 40 in.
© Estate of Larry Sultan

XI. Advertisements

APRIL 1 - JUNE 1, 2019

RECEPTION MAY 2ND 5-9PM

EMILY ABSTRACTED

WILLIAM T HILLMAN

AFFIRMATION ARTS

523 WEST 37TH STREET NEW YORK, NY 11204

212-925-0092 INFO@AFFIRMATIONARTS.COM

OPEN BY APPOINTMENT

photograph magazine
is dedicated to photo-based art,
offering essential, insightful
coverage of exhibitions, people,
ideas, books, events, and resources.

A one year subscription:
$35/US, $40/Canada,
$70/all other countries.
Payment by check, AmEx,
MC, Visa or PayPal at
photographmag.com/subscribe.

Want a weekly round-up
of what's going on?
Sign up for our newsletter
with updates on openings,
news, reviews, and more at
photographmag.com

f photographmagazine   **𝕏** **📷** @photographmag

photograph

MARCH/APRIL 2019 $5.

©Don Worth, *Water Drops, San Francisco*, 1960. Courtesy Scott Nichols Gallery

One company, full-service, trusted worldwide since 1996

Official Shipping Company of The Photography Show

Enjoy peace of mind while our dedicated
specialists facilitate the handling and
shipping of your fine art with
the professional knowledge and
respect it deserves

Thank you AIPAD for placing your trust in us

📞 +1-516-825-5885 | ✉ estimates@aetnafineart.com | 🖥 AetnaFineArt.com
New York

"Creativity
Takes
Courage"
—HENRI MATISSE

Be Brave.

Edward Steichen, *Crewmen hastily
drag plane with flat tire down flight
deck of* USS Lexington (CV-16) *to
make way for next plane to land,* 1943.

ArtandObject.com

Art&object

Bonhams

AUCTIONEERS SINCE 1793

Photographs

New York | April 5, 2019

PREVIEW
March 30- April 5

INQUIRIES
Laura Paterson
+1 (917) 206 1653
laura.paterson@bonhams.com
bonhams.com/photos

FRANCESCA WOODMAN
*Francesca Woodman,
Providence, Rhode Island*,
1975-1978
Gelatin Silver Print, from the
edition of 40.
7 7/8 x 10in (19.9 x 25.4cm)
$10,000 - 15,000

© 2019 Bonhams & Butterfields Auctioneers Corp. All rights reserved. Principal Auctioneer: Matthew Girling, NYC License No. 1236798-DCA

Photography Auction
in Berlin 29 May 2019

Albert Renger–Patzsch. Power Centre of a Locomotive. 1925. Vintage. Gelatin silver print. 6⅝ × 8¼ in. © VG Bild-Kunst, Bonn 2019. Estimate EUR 40.000–60.000

GRISEBACH

Diandra Donecker, Photography
T +49 30 885 915 27
Fasanenstrasse 25, 10719 Berlin
grisebach.com

PHOTOGRAPHS
April 6 | New York | Live & Online

Including an Important Collection of Ruth Bernhard Photographs

RUTH BERNHARD (American, 1905-2006)
Perspective II, 1967
Gelatin silver
Estimate: $4,000 - $6,000

View | Track | Bid
HA.com/5409

Inquiries:
Nigel Russell
NigelR@HA.com | 212.486.3659

HERITAGE
AUCTIONS
AMERICA'S AUCTION HOUSE

DALLAS | NEW YORK | BEVERLY HILLS | SAN FRANCISCO | CHICAGO | PALM BEACH
LONDON | PARIS | GENEVA | AMSTERDAM | HONG KONG

Paul R. Minshull #16591. BP 12-25%; see HA.com 53211

Celebrating
the Arts

Sidley is a proud sponsor of

THE
PHOTOGRAPHY
SHOW

As a global law firm with a rich history
of supporting the visual arts, we
are pleased to join with AIPAD in
celebrating the best in fine photography
and bringing together a community
of exceptional artists, collectors and
advocates of this dynamic medium.

SIDLEY

AMERICA • ASIA PACIFIC • EUROPE
sidley.com

Attorney Advertising - Sidley Austin LLP, One South Dearborn, Chicago, IL 60603.
+1 312 853 7000. Prior results do not guarantee a similar outcome. MN-10226

Photographs

AUCTION NEW YORK 5 APRIL

EL LISSITZKY
Pelikan Tinte, 1924
Estimate $300,000–500,000

EXHIBITION FREE AND OPEN TO THE PUBLIC 29 MARCH–4 APRIL

1334 YORK AVENUE, NEW YORK, NY 10021
ENQUIRIES +1 212 894 1149   PHOTOGRAPHSNY@SOTHEBYS.COM
SOTHEBYS.COM/PHOTOGRAPHS   #SOTHEBYSPHOTOGRAPHS
© 2019 ARTISTS RIGHTS SOCIETY (ARS), NEW YORK / VG BILD-KUNST, BONN

DOWNLOAD SOTHEBY'S APP
FOLLOW US @SOTHEBYS

SWANN
AUCTION GALLERIES

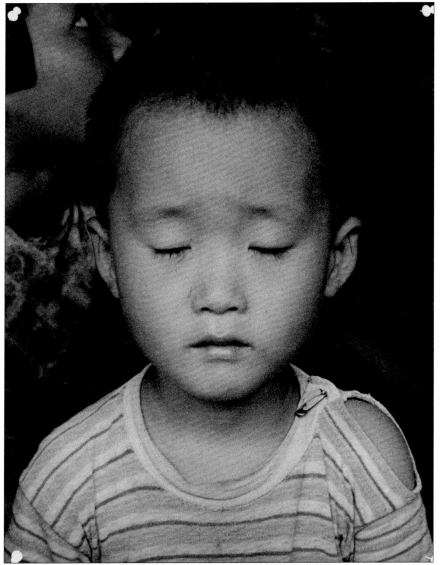

Dorothea Lange, *Korean Child*, silver print, 1958, printed 1960s. Estimate $20,000 to $30,000.

Classic & Contemporary Photographs
April 18

Daile Kaplan • dkaplan@swanngalleries.com

Download the App

104 E 25th Street, NYC • 212 254 4710 • SWANNGALLERIES.COM

When Art meets Beauty

Created in 1985 Valmont is an anti-aging Swiss skincare brand using triple DNA, cutting edge technology and pure resources that deliver immediate, visible and long lasting results. Owner and Creative Director Didier Guillon's passion for art is the umbrella that covers the entire Valmont Group.

This 360-degree view of beauty has helped create La Fondation Valmont, whose goal is to share with a large public the passion for art and beauty.

Valmont is very proud to be a partner of The Photography Show.

www.valmontcosmetics.com

Archival Storage and Presentation Products

AIPAD MEMBERS SAVE 20% WITH CODE #12749

ARCHIVALMETHODS.COM

BASSENGE

PHOTOGRAPHY AUCTIONS

PHOTOGRAPHY AUCTION
JUNE 2019

Consignments now welcome!

Erdener Str. 5A | 14193 Berlin | Germany
Phone +49 30 21 99 72 77 | Fax +49 30 21 99 71 05
jennifer@bassenge.com | www.bassenge.com

AUGUST SANDER
Portrait of a young confirmand.
1910s. Vintage matte gelatin silver print.
Sold for 42,800 Euro

Photography requires a special kind of insurance.

We focus on the details.

DeWitt Stern
Insurance & Risk Advisory | Since 1899
A DIVISION OF RISK STRATEGIES

Mpontillo@dewittstern.com
212.297.1420

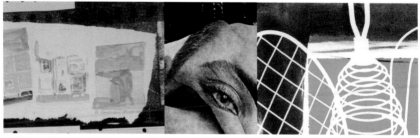

The Path of Darryl Curran: From the 1960s - the Present
(and the Origins of Cameraless Photography)
Also exhibiting influences by Robert Heineken, Todd Walker, Betty Hahn and more.
January 11 - February 29, 2020

dnj

www.dnjgallery.net
3015 Ocean Park Blvd
Santa Monica, CA 90405

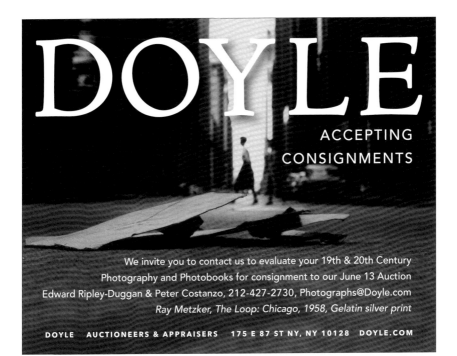

DOYLE

ACCEPTING
CONSIGNMENTS

We invite you to contact us to evaluate your 19th & 20th Century
Photography and Photobooks for consignment to our June 13 Auction
Edward Ripley-Duggan & Peter Costanzo, 212-427-2730, Photographs@Doyle.com
Ray Metzker, The Loop: Chicago, 1958, Gelatin silver print

DOYLE   AUCTIONEERS & APPRAISERS   175 E 87 ST NY, NY 10128   DOYLE.COM

galleryintell

PROFESSIONAL VIDEO PRODUCTION
WITH FOCUS ON THE ARTS

SINCE 2012

VIDEO@GALLERYINTELL.COM

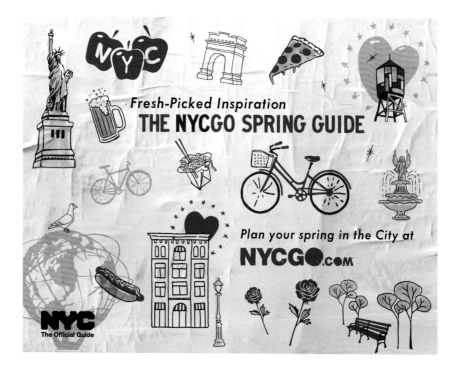

Fresh-Picked Inspiration
THE NYCGO SPRING GUIDE

Plan your spring in the City at
NYCGO.com

NYC
The Official Guide

PAUL MESSIER LLC
Conservation of Photographs & Works on Paper
Serving institutional and private clients worldwide since 1994

Boston, MA   www.paulmessier.com   617.782.7110

Ꝓ PENELOPE DIXON & ASSOCIATES

Providing premier appraisals of documentary, commercial
and fine art photography worldwide since 1981

- First appraisers to be certified solely in photography.

- Specializing in appraisals of collections both small and large
  for the purpose of insurance, donation, estate taxes and sales.

- Leading provider in appraisals of archives & estates.

- USPAP compliant and certified members of the
  Appraisers Association of America.

peneloped.com

Please visit our website for a complete listing of our extensive services and resources.
877-837-2777 | info@peneloped.com

SKINNER

Fine Photographs at auction

Inviting consignments   photographs@skinnerinc.com   508.970.3206

Nan Goldin (American, b. 1953) *Greer and Robert on the Bed, New York*, 1982, sold for $12,300   I   MA LIC. 2304

Boston | Marlborough | Miami | New York | www.skinnerinc.com

JOHN ADAM STASZYN

325 East 21st Street, Suite 11, New York, N.Y. 10010

PHOTOGRAPHY APPRAISALS

Professional Appraisals of Photographs
Insurance, Estate and Donation Purposes
Uniform Standards of Professional Appraisal Practices

jedzyn@aol.com

tel/fax (212) 260-6350

APPRAISALS *Donations of fine art photographs to museums and institutions continue to hold special benefits. We are pleased to provide appraisal services for donation, insurance, estate planning and other purposes.*

APPRAISALS & CONSULTATIONS **Stulz**

5441 West 138th Place
Hawthorne, California 90250
Phone: 310-643-0202
Fax: 310-643-0292

CONSULTATIONS *Consulting services are also available to private, corporate and institutional collections in acquiring and deaccessioning photographs and other works of art.*

For furthur information please contact

Dale W. Stulz
Since 1951

LOS ANGELES   NEW YORK   LONDON   PARIS   COLOGNE   TOKYO   SAN FRANCISCO   CHICAGO   HOUSTON   ATLANTA

Index

Lola Álvarez Bravo
Charles Isaacs Photography, Inc.,
Throckmorton Fine Art, Inc.

Manuel Álvarez Bravo
Catherine Couturier Gallery, Charles Isaacs
Photography, Inc., Contemporary Works/
Vintage Works, Etherton Gallery, The Halsted
Gallery, Hyperion Press, Ltd., Michael
Shapiro Photographs, Paul M. Hertzmann,
Inc., Robert Koch Gallery, Scheinbaum &
Russek, Ltd., Throckmorton Fine Art, Inc.,
William L. Schaeffer Photographic Works
of Art

James Anderson
Gary Edwards Gallery

Keliy Anderson-Staley
Catherine Edelman Gallery

Juliette Andrea-Elie
baudoin lebon gallery

Holly Andres
Robert Koch Gallery, Robert Mann Gallery

Ljubodrag Andric
Robert Koch Gallery

Sara Angelucci
Stephen Bulger Gallery

Roswell Angier
Gitterman Gallery

Peter Anton Unix Gallery
Takashi Arai PGI

Nobuyoshi Araki
Michael Hoppen Gallery

Diane Arbus
ClampArt, Etherton Gallery, Fraenkel
Gallery, Jörg Maaß Kunsthandel, Robert
Mann Gallery

Anne Arden McDonald
Candela Gallery

Bill Armstrong
ClampArt, HackelBury Fine Art

David Armstrong
ClampArt

Steven Arnold
Fahey/Klein Gallery

John Arsenault
ClampArt

Alexander Artway
Stephen Bulger Gallery

Mar Arza
RocioSantaCruz

Kiichi Asano
Scott Nichols Gallery

Morgan Ashcom
Candela Gallery

Ananké Asseff
Rolf Art

Eugène Atget
Alan Klotz Gallery, Barry Singer Gallery,
Charles Isaacs Photography, Inc.,
GALLERY 19/21, Hans P. Kraus Jr.
Inc., Hyperion Press, Ltd., Lee Gallery,
L. Parker Stephenson Photographs,
Paul M. Hertzmann, Inc., Robert Koch
Gallery, Scheinbaum & Russek, Ltd., Scott
Nichols Gallery

Anna Atkins
Hans P. Kraus Jr. Inc., Lee Gallery

Jane Evelyn Atwood
L. Parker Stephenson Photographs

Ellen Auerbach
Robert Mann Gallery

Jacob Aue Sobol
Polka Galerie

Index

Richard Avedon
Fraenkel Gallery, Pace/MacGill Gallery, Staley-Wise Gallery

Sid Avery
Staley-Wise Gallery

Kristoffer Axen
Fahey/Klein Gallery

Aziz + Cucher
ClampArt

Morley Baer
Scott Nichols Gallery

Clara Bahlsen
Galerie f5,6

Fatemeh Baigmoradi
LAURENCE MILLER GALLERY

Patrick Bailly-Maitre-Grand
baudoin lebon gallery

John Baldessari
Barry Singer Gallery

Édouard Baldus
Gary Edwards Gallery, Hans P. Kraus Jr. Inc., James Hyman Gallery, Robert Koch Gallery

Roger Ballen
Barry Singer Gallery, Elizabeth Houston Gallery, Etherton Gallery, Fahey/Klein Gallery, Robert Koch Gallery

Pauline Ballet
In The Gallery

Dmitri Baltermants
Etherton Gallery

Lewis Baltz
Joseph Bellows Gallery, Lee Gallery, Paul M. Hertzmann, Inc.

Olivo Barbieri
Yancey Richardson Gallery

Anthony Barboza
Keith de Lellis Gallery

Tom Baril
Fahey/Klein Gallery, Hyperion Press, Ltd., Robert Koch Gallery

Jared Bark
Yancey Richardson Gallery

Agnes Barley
Sears-Peyton Gallery

Bruce Barnbaum
Fahey/Klein Gallery

Yto Barrada
Pace/MacGill Gallery

Thomas Barrow
Joseph Bellows Gallery

Mary Ellen Bartley
Yancey Richardson Gallery

Adam Bartos
Gitterman Gallery

Peter Basch
Fahey/Klein Gallery, Henry Feldstein, Staley-Wise Gallery

Lillian Bassman
Edwynn Houk Gallery, Galerie f5,6, Staley-Wise Gallery

Elmer Batters
Henry Feldstein

Bauhaus
Kicken Berlin

Ernesto Bazan
Sous Les Etoiles Gallery

Virginia Beahan
Joseph Bellows Gallery

John Beasley Greene
Contemporary Works/Vintage Works,
GILLES PEYROULET & CIE

Felice Beato
Gary Edwards Gallery, Robert Koch Gallery

Cecil Beaton
Augusta Edwards Fine Art, Keith de Lellis
Gallery, Staley-Wise Gallery

Bernd & Hilla Becher
Bruce Silverstein Gallery, Fraenkel Gallery,
Kicken Berlin

Olaf Otto Becker
ClampArt, Galerie f5,6, Huxley-
Parlour Gallery

Janette Beckman
Fahey/Klein Gallery

Jeffrey Becom
Lee Marks Fine Art

Josh Begley
Robert Koch Gallery

Valérie Belin
Edwynn Houk Gallery, Huxley-Parlour Gallery

William Bell
Richard Moore Photographs, William L.
Schaeffer Photographic Works of Art

Jaret Belliveau
Stephen Bulger Gallery

Hans Bellmer
Hyperion Press, Ltd.

Daniel Beltrá
Catherine Edelman Gallery

Ernest Benecke
Gary Edwards Gallery

Carolle Benitah
Sous Les Etoiles Gallery

Harry Benson
Fahey/Klein Gallery, GALERIE FRÉDÉRIC
GOT, Holden Luntz Gallery, Inc., Monroe
Gallery of Photography, Staley-Wise Gallery

Michael Benson
Flowers Gallery

Sibylle Bergemann
Kicken Berlin

Damion Berger
Lisa Sette Gallery

Phil Bergerson
Stephen Bulger Gallery

Ladislav Berka
GILLES PEYROULET & CIE

Ferenc Berko
Gitterman Gallery

Michael Berman
Etherton Gallery

Nina Berman
Monroe Gallery of Photography

Mathieu Bernard-Reymond
baudoin lebon gallery

Ruth Bernhard
Etherton Gallery, The Halsted Gallery,
Robert Koch Gallery, Scott Nichols Gallery,
Wach Gallery

Index

Isaac H. Bonsall
Contemporary Works/Vintage Works

Boogie
Laufer

Boomoon
Flowers Gallery

Alvin Booth
Fahey/Klein Gallery

Andrew Borowiec
Alan Klotz Gallery, Lee Marks Fine Art

Julie Boserup
Sous Les Etoiles Gallery

Henry P. Bosse
Lee Gallery

Enrique Bostelmann
Toluca Fine Art

Machiel Botman
Gitterman Gallery

Edouard Boubat
Contemporary Works/Vintage Works,
GALLERY 19/21, Hyperion Press, Ltd.

Alfredo Boulton
Toluca Fine Art

Robert Bourdeau
Stephen Bulger Gallery

Guy Bourdin
Louise Alexander Gallery

Margaret Bourke-White
Alan Klotz Gallery, Keith de Lellis Gallery,
Michael Shapiro Photographs, Monroe
Gallery of Photography, Richard Moore
Photographs, Wach Gallery, William L.
Schaeffer Photographic Works of Art

Samuel Bourne
Gary Edwards Gallery

Rémi Bourquin
GALERIE FRÉDÉRIC GOT

Marcel Bovis
Contemporary Works/Vintage Works

Justin Bower
Unix Gallery

Boyd & Evans
Flowers Gallery

William Bradley
Unix Gallery

Bragagia Brothers
Hyperion Press, Ltd.

Anton Giulio Bragaglia
Robert Koch Gallery

Constantin Brancusi
Bruce Silverstein Gallery, Kicken Berlin,
Robert Koch Gallery

Malthe Brandenburg
In The Gallery

Barbara Brandli
Charles Isaacs Photography, Inc.

Bill Brandt
Atlas Gallery, Contemporary Works/Vintage
Works, The Halsted Gallery, James Hyman
Gallery, Jörg Maaß Kunsthandel, Paul M.
Hertzmann, Inc., Robert Koch Gallery

Nick Brandt
Atlas Gallery, Edwynn Houk Gallery, Fahey/
Klein Gallery

Bruno-Auguste Braquehais
Contemporary Works/Vintage Works

Index

Susan Burnstine
Catherine Couturier Gallery

René Burri
Atlas Gallery

Larry Burrows
LAURENCE MILLER GALLERY

Nancy Burson
ClampArt, Contemporary Works/
Vintage Works

Wendy Burton
Lee Marks Fine Art

Edward Burtynsky
Bryce Wolkowitz Gallery, Flowers Gallery,
Howard Greenberg Gallery, Robert Koch
Gallery, Weinstein Hammons Gallery

Albarrán Cabrera
IBASHO

Debbie Fleming Caffery
Gitterman Gallery

Robert Calafiore
ClampArt

Richard Caldicott
Atlas Gallery, Sous Les Etoiles Gallery

Harry Callahan
Alan Klotz Gallery, Contemporary Works/
Vintage Works, Etherton Gallery, The Halsted
Gallery, Jackson Fine Art, James Hyman
Gallery, Jörg Maaß Kunsthandel, Joseph
Bellows Gallery, LAURENCE MILLER
GALLERY, Michael Shapiro Photographs,
Pace/MacGill Gallery, Paul M. Hertzmann,
Inc., Robert Mann Gallery, Scheinbaum &
Russek, Ltd., Scott Nichols Gallery

Sophie Calle
Fraenkel Gallery

Johanna Calle
Toluca Fine Art

Camera Work
Scheinbaum & Russek, Ltd.

Julia Margaret Cameron
Alan Klotz Gallery, Charles Isaacs
Photography, Inc., Contemporary Works/
Vintage Works, Hans P. Kraus Jr. Inc., Robert
Koch Gallery

Jim Campbell
Bryce Wolkowitz Gallery

Luca Campigotto
LAURENCE MILLER GALLERY

Giacomo Caneva
Charles Isaacs Photography, Inc.,
Contemporary Works/Vintage Works

Cornell Capa
The Halsted Gallery

Robert Capa
Henry Feldstein, The Halsted Gallery

Paul Caponigro
Catherine Couturier Gallery, Etherton
Gallery, Joseph Bellows Gallery, Scheinbaum
& Russek, Ltd., Scott Nichols Gallery

Luiz Carlos Felizardo
Utópica

Index

Lucien Clergue
La Galerie de l'Instant, Throckmorton Fine Art, Inc.

Charles Clifford
Contemporary Works/Vintage Works, GILLES PEYROULET & CIE, Robert Koch Gallery

William Clift
Joseph Bellows Gallery, Scheinbaum & Russek, Ltd., Scott Nichols Gallery

Alvin L. Coburn
Paul M. Hertzmann, Inc.

Daniel W. Coburn
Elizabeth Houston Gallery

Robert Coburn
Fahey/Klein Gallery

Julie Cockburn
Flowers Gallery

John Cohen
L. Parker Stephenson Photographs

Lynne Cohen
Stephen Daiter Gallery

Van Deren Coke
Scheinbaum & Russek, Ltd.

Christopher Colville
Etherton Gallery

Nicolas Comment
Polka Galerie

Scott Conarroe
Stephen Bulger Gallery

Jeffrey Conley
Peter Fetterman Gallery

Linda Connor
Candela Gallery, Etherton Gallery, Joseph Bellows Gallery, Scheinbaum & Russek, Ltd.

Lois Conner
Gitterman Gallery

Gregory Conniff
Joseph Bellows Gallery

Dimitri Constantine
Gary Edwards Gallery

Mariana Cook
Deborah Bell Photographs, Lee Marks Fine Art

Allen Cooley
Arnika Dawkins Gallery Photographic Fine Art

Nicholas Cope
Fahey/Klein Gallery

John Coplans
Contemporary Works/Vintage Works, Joseph Bellows Gallery

Cristina Coral
Momentum Fine Art

Pierre Cordier
HackelBury Fine Art

Sharon Core
Yancey Richardson Gallery

Richard Corman
Peter Fetterman Gallery

Carlotta Corpron
PDNB Gallery

Cortis & Sonderegger
Bryce Wolkowitz Gallery

Gordon Coster
Keith de Lellis Gallery

Index

D

Judy Dater
Etherton Gallery, Scheinbaum & Russek, Ltd., Scott Nichols Gallery

Siân Davey
Michael Hoppen Gallery

Bruce Davidson
Catherine Edelman Gallery, Howard Greenberg Gallery, Huxley-Parlour Gallery, Jackson Fine Art, William L. Schaeffer Photographic Works of Art

Bevan Davies
Joseph Bellows Gallery

John Davies
L. Parker Stephenson Photographs

Jen Davis
ClampArt, Lee Marks Fine Art

Lynn Davis
Edwynn Houk Gallery

Joe Deal
Robert Mann Gallery

Max Dean
Stephen Bulger Gallery

Geraldo de Barros
Augusta Edwards Fine Art

Louis de Clercq
Contemporary Works/Vintage Works, Robert Koch Gallery

Liliane De Cock
Scheinbaum & Russek, Ltd.

Luuk de Haan
Sous Les Etoiles Gallery

Gerry Deiter
Stephen Bulger Gallery

Jack Delano
PDNB Gallery, Richard Moore Photographs

James Whitlow Delano
Sous Les Etoiles Gallery

Sophie Delaporte
Sous Les Etoiles Gallery

Floriane de Lassée
Catherine Edelman Gallery

Milagros de la Torre
Rolf Art, Toluca Fine Art

Alphonse De Launay
Contemporary Works/Vintage Works

Sonia Delaunay
BOCCARA ART

Patrick Demarchelier
Fahey/Klein Gallery, Staley-Wise Gallery

Ellen de Meijer
Unix Gallery

Jean Denant
RocioSantaCruz

Monica Denevan
Scott Nichols Gallery

Frances F. Denny
ClampArt

Wijnanda Deroo
Robert Mann Gallery

Marquis De Rostaing
Contemporary Works/Vintage Works

Thomas Deutschmann
Kicken Berlin

Lucinda Devlin
Lee Marks Fine Art

Index

Louis-Émile Durandelle
Contemporary Works/Vintage Works, Robert Koch Gallery

Stéphane Duroy
only photography

Jay Dusard
Etherton Gallery

Michael Dweck
Fahey/Klein Gallery, Staley-Wise Gallery

E

William Eakin
Stephen Bulger Gallery

Thomas Eakins
Contemporary Works/Vintage Works

Michael Eastman
Edwynn Houk Gallery, Lisa Sette Gallery, Robert Koch Gallery

Harold Edgerton
Etherton Gallery, Robert Koch Gallery, Scott Nichols Gallery

William Eggleston
Jörg Maaß Kunsthandel, PDNB Gallery

Josef Ehm
Contemporary Works/Vintage Works, Robert Koch Gallery

Alfred Ehrhardt
Kicken Berlin

Frauke Eigen
Atlas Gallery, only photography

Ei-Q
Paul M. Hertzmann, Inc.

Juliane Eirich
Galerie f5,6

Alfred Eisenstaedt
Contemporary Works/Vintage Works, Monroe Gallery of Photography, Winter Works on Paper

Adam Ekberg
ClampArt

Liat Elbling
Catherine Edelman Gallery

Arthur Elgort
Atlas Gallery, Fahey/Klein Gallery, Staley-Wise Gallery

Eliot Elisofon
Gitterman Gallery

Martin Elkort
Catherine Couturier Gallery

Gonzalo Elvira
RocioSantaCruz

Peter Henry Emerson
Alan Klotz Gallery, Robert Koch Gallery

Morris Engel
The Halsted Gallery, PDNB Gallery, Richard Moore Photographs

Bill Eppridge
Monroe Gallery of Photography

Mitch Epstein
Yancey Richardson Gallery

Hugo Erfurth
Kicken Berlin

Robert Erickson Estate
PDNB Gallery

Index

F

Barry Feinstein
Fahey/Klein Gallery

Harold Feinstein
PDNB Gallery

Denis Felix
GALERIE FRÉDÉRIC GOT

Tom Fels
Atlas Gallery

Christopher Felver
Fahey/Klein Gallery

Roger Fenton
Charles Isaacs Photography, Inc., Hans
P. Kraus Jr. Inc., William L. Schaeffer
Photographic Works of Art

Ferenc Ficzek
Robert Koch Gallery

Gerard Fieret
Deborah Bell Photographs, Paul M.
Hertzmann, Inc.

Gabriel Figueroa
Charles Isaacs Photography, Inc.

John Filo
Monroe Gallery of Photography

Brian Finke
ClampArt

Amy Finkelstein
Elizabeth Houston Gallery

Richard Finkelstein
Robert Mann Gallery

Arno Fischer
Kicken Berlin

Alida Fish
Alan Klotz Gallery

Steve Fitch
Robert Koch Gallery

Robbert Flick
Joseph Bellows Gallery, Robert Mann Gallery

John Florea Estate
Fahey/Klein Gallery

Lucas Foglia
Michael Hoppen Gallery

Folkwang Auriga Verlag
Kicken Berlin

Mario Fonseca
Augusta Edwards Fine Art

Franco Fontana
baudoin lebon gallery

Nancy Ford Cones
Contemporary Works/Vintage Works

Ivan Forde
De Soto Gallery

Formento & Formento
Fahey/Klein Gallery, Momentum Fine Art

Jody Forster
Etherton Gallery

Francois Alphonse Fortier
Contemporary Works/Vintage Works

Foto Ada
Robert Koch Gallery

Foto Cine Clube Bandeirante
Utópica

fotoform
Kicken Berlin

Anna Fox
James Hyman Gallery

Index

Allen Frame
Gitterman Gallery

Martine Franck
Augusta Edwards Fine Art

Fernell Franco
Toluca Fine Art

Dorian François
baudoin lebon gallery

Robert Frank
Alan Klotz Gallery, Barry Singer Gallery,
Contemporary Works/Vintage Works,
Edwynn Houk Gallery, Etherton Gallery,
Gitterman Gallery, Jörg Maaß Kunsthandel,
Pace/MacGill Gallery, Paul M. Hertzmann,
Inc., Robert Mann Gallery

Tony Frank
La Galerie de l'Instant

Stuart Franklin
Augusta Edwards Fine Art, Galerie Catherine
et André Hug

Manuel Franquelo
Michael Hoppen Gallery

Murray Fredericks
Robert Mann Gallery

Charles Fréger
Kicken Berlin, MEM, Inc.

Jean-Baptiste Frénet
GALLERY 19/21

Lee Friedlander
Contemporary Works/Vintage Works,
Etherton Gallery, Fraenkel Gallery, Winter
Works on Paper

Toni Frissell
Staley-Wise Gallery

Francis Frith
Contemporary Works/Vintage Works, Robert
Koch Gallery

Louis-Antoine Froissart
Hans P. Kraus Jr. Inc.

Monique Frydman
BOCCARA ART

Hitoshi Fugo
IBASHO

Masahisa Fukase
Michael Hoppen Gallery, Robert
Mann Gallery

Shihoko Fukumoto
MEM, Inc.

Jane Fulton Alt
Sous Les Etoiles Gallery

Jaromír Funke
Kicken Berlin, Robert Koch Gallery

Adam Fuss
Fraenkel Gallery

Charles Gagnon
Stephen Bulger Gallery

Vivian Galban
Rolf Art

Andrés Galeano
RocioSantaCruz

Ron Galella
Staley-Wise Gallery

Sally Gall
Robert Klein Gallery

Héctor García
Charles Isaacs Photography, Inc.,
Throckmorton Fine Art, Inc.

Ana Garcia-Pineda
RocioSantaCruz

Ferran Garcia Sevilla
RocioSantaCruz

Gilbert Garcin
Lisa Sette Gallery, Stephen Bulger Gallery

Alexander Gardner
Lee Gallery

Flor Garduño
Etherton Gallery, Fahey/Klein Gallery,
Throckmorton Fine Art, Inc.

Richard Garet
Unix Gallery

William Garnett
Joseph Bellows Gallery, Paul M. Hertzmann,
Inc., Richard Moore Photographs,
Scheinbaum & Russek, Ltd., Scott
Nichols Gallery

Gaspar Gasparian
Augusta Edwards Fine Art

Paolo Gasparini
Toluca Fine Art

Jean Gasperd Roman
Contemporary Works/Vintage Works

William Gedney
L. Parker Stephenson Photographs

Lynn Geesaman
Scheinbaum & Russek, Ltd.

Andreas Gefeller
Atlas Gallery, Sous Les Etoiles Gallery

Judy Gelles
De Soto Gallery

André Gelpke
Kicken Berlin

Arnold Genthe
Paul M. Hertzmann, Inc., Robert Koch Gallery

Celia Gerard
Sears-Peyton Gallery

Kathleen Gerber
Catherine Edelman Gallery, ClampArt

Richard Gere
Fahey/Klein Gallery

Ori Gersht
Yancey Richardson Gallery

Lynn Gessaman
Yancey Richardson Gallery

Mario Giacomelli
Contemporary Works/Vintage Works,
GALLERY 19/21, Keith de Lellis Gallery,
Polka Galerie, Robert Koch Gallery, Robert
Mann Gallery

Antonio Giannuzzi
Contemporary Works/Vintage Works

Robert Giard
Stephen Bulger Gallery

David H. Gibson
Wach Gallery

Index

Bryan Graf
Yancey Richardson Gallery

François Gragnon
La Galerie de l'Instant

David Graham
Etherton Gallery, LAURENCE MILLER
GALLERY, PDNB Gallery

Paul Graham
Pace/MacGill Gallery

Katy Grannan
Fraenkel Gallery

Ken Grant
James Hyman Gallery

Edward Grazda
Deborah Bell Photographs

Jill Greenberg
ClampArt

John B. Greene
Gary Edwards Gallery, Hans P. Kraus Jr. Inc.,
Lee Gallery, Robert Koch Gallery

Milton H. Greene
La Galerie de l'Instant, Staley-Wise Gallery

Lauren Greenfield
Fahey/Klein Gallery, Robert Koch Gallery

Cynthia Greig
Stephen Bulger Gallery

William Greiner
PDNB Gallery

Brian Griffin
James Hyman Gallery

Alexander Gronsky
Polka Galerie

Walter Grossman
Wach Gallery

Bob Gruen
Fahey/Klein Gallery

Torkil Gudnason
Fahey/Klein Gallery

Phillipe Guionie
Polka Galerie

F.C. Gundlach
Kicken Berlin

Sunil Gupta
Stephen Bulger Gallery

John Gutmann
Winter Works on Paper

Beate Gutschow
Augusta Edwards Fine Art

Janice Guy
Yancey Richardson Gallery

Holics Gyula
GALLERY 19/21

Ferenc Haar
Robert Koch Gallery

Ernst Haas
Atlas Gallery, Monroe Gallery of
Photography, Wach Gallery

Index

Dave Heath
Barry Singer Gallery, Howard Greenberg Gallery, Stephen Bulger Gallery

Erik Madigan
Heck Jackson Fine Art, Weinstein Hammons Gallery

Walter Hege
Kicken Berlin

Emil Heilborn
Robert Mann Gallery

Kenneth Heilbron
Contemporary Works/Vintage Works

Jean-Jacques Heilmann
Contemporary Works/Vintage Works

Robert Heinecken
Barry Singer Gallery, Contemporary Works/ Vintage Works, Paul M. Hertzmann, Inc., Robert Koch Gallery

Annemarie Heinrich
Utópica

William Helburn
Staley-Wise Gallery

Beatrice Helg
Joel Soroka Gallery

Fritz Henle
Throckmorton Fine Art, Inc.

Mishka Henner
Bruce Silverstein Gallery

Florence Henri
Atlas Gallery, Robert Koch Gallery

Matt Henry
Polka Galerie

James Herbert
Gitterman Gallery

Jorge Heredia
Toluca Fine Art

Anthony Hernandez
Yancey Richardson Gallery

Fred Herzog
LAURENCE MILLER GALLERY

Todd Hido
Bruce Silverstein Gallery

Chester Higgins Jr.
Scott Nichols Gallery

Hill & Adamson
Charles Isaacs Photography, Inc., Contemporary Works/Vintage Works, Hans P. Kraus Jr. Inc., Robert Koch Gallery

Paul Hill
James Hyman Gallery, L. Parker Stephenson Photographs

Richard Scott Hill
Richard Moore Photographs

John Karl Hillers
Paul M. Hertzmann, Inc., Robert Koch Gallery

David Hilliard
Yancey Richardson Gallery

Paul Himmel
Galerie f5,6

Lewis Hine
Alan Klotz Gallery, Contemporary Works/ Vintage Works, Joel Soroka Gallery, Paul M. Hertzmann, Inc., Richard Moore Photographs

Nicholas C. Hlobeczy
Wach Gallery

Hannah Höch
Kicken Berlin

Index

John Humble
Joseph Bellows Gallery

Tom Hunter
Yancey Richardson Gallery

George Hurrell
Fahey/Klein Gallery, Scott Nichols Gallery,
Staley-Wise Gallery

David Husom
Joseph Bellows Gallery

Carl Austin Hyatt
Wach Gallery

I

Patricia Iglesias
Sears-Peyton Gallery

Boris Ignatovich
Robert Koch Gallery

Yoko Ikeda
IBASHO, LAURENCE MILLER GALLERY

Omar Imam
Catherine Edelman Gallery

Tolla Inbar
GALERIE FRÉDÉRIC GOT

Vid Ingelevics
Stephen Bulger Gallery

Carsten Ingemann
In The Gallery

Stephen Inggs
HackelBury Fine Art

Walter Iooss
Fahey/Klein Gallery

Pello Irazu
Yancey Richardson Gallery

Hideyuki Ishibashi
IBASHO

Tomoaki Ishihara
MEM, Inc.

Yasuhiro Ishimoto
Contemporary Works/Vintage Works,
GALLERY 19/21, IBASHO, PGI

Yoshihiko Ito
PGI

Graciela Iturbide
Etherton Gallery, Throckmorton Fine Art,
Inc., Toluca Fine Art

Izis
Contemporary Works/Vintage Works, L.
Parker Stephenson Photographs.

Kenro Izu
Scheinbaum & Russek, Ltd.

Yumiko Izu
Scheinbaum & Russek, Ltd

Ayana V. Jackson
baudoin lebon gallery

Thomas Jackson
Jackson Fine Art

Index

K

Miho Kajioka
IBASHO

Simpson Kalisher
Keith de Lellis Gallery

Consuelo Kanaga
Michael Shapiro Photographs

Nadav Kander
Flowers Gallery

Osamu Kanemura
only photography

Hyun Ae Kang
BOCCARA ART

Airan Kang
Bryce Wolkowitz Gallery

Ruth Kaplan
Stephen Bulger Gallery

Sid Kaplan
Deborah Bell Photographs

Yousuf Karsh
Fahey/Klein Gallery, The Halsted Gallery,
Huxley-Parlour Gallery, Robert Klein Gallery,
Robert Koch Gallery, Scott Nichols Gallery,
Wach Gallery, Yancey Richardson Gallery

Gertrude Käsebier
Lee Gallery, Richard Moore Photographs

Barbara Kasten
Contemporary Works/Vintage Works

Adam Katseff
Robert Koch Gallery

Jimmy & Dena Katz
PDNB Gallery

Kikuji Kawada
L. Parker Stephenson Photographs, PGI

Zhang Kechun
Huxley-Parlour Gallery, Robert Mann Gallery

Minna Keene
Stephen Bulger Gallery

Violet Keene Perinchief
Stephen Bulger Gallery

Peter Keetman
Jörg Maaß Kunsthandel, Kicken Berlin,
only photography

Oli Kellett
HackelBury Fine Art

Michael Kenna
Catherine Couturier Gallery, Catherine
Edelman Gallery, The Halsted Gallery,
Huxley-Parlour Gallery, Paul M. Hertzmann,
Inc., PDNB Gallery, Robert Mann Gallery,
Scheinbaum & Russek, Ltd., Scott
Nichols Gallery

György Kepes
Joel Soroka Gallery, L. Parker Stephenson
Photographs, Robert Klein Gallery, Robert
Koch Gallery, Stephen Daiter Gallery

Wang Keping
BOCCARA ART

Gábor Kerekes
Stephen Bulger Gallery

Lisa Kereszi
Yancey Richardson Gallery

Geof Kern
Fahey/Klein Gallery, PDNB Gallery

Pascal Kern
HackelBury Fine Art

Sean Kernan
GALLERY 19/21

Index

Karen Knorr
Augusta Edwards Fine Art, Holden Luntz
Gallery, Inc.

Heinrich Koch
Kicken Berlin

Yasue Kodama
MEM, Inc.

Michael Koerner
Catherine Edelman Gallery

Viktor Kolár
only photography, Stephen Bulger Gallery

Bernice Kolko
Charles Isaacs Photography, Inc.

François Kollar
Contemporary Works/Vintage
Works, GALLERY 19/21, GILLES
PEYROULET & CIE

Michiko Kon
PGI, Robert Mann Gallery

Toru Kono
MEM, Inc.

Sirkka-Liisa Konttinen
L. Parker Stephenson Photographs

Rudolf Koppitz
Kicken Berlin

Alberto Korda Estate
Sous Les Etoiles Gallery

Nina Korhonen
Lee Marks Fine Art

August Kotzsch
Kicken Berlin

Josef Koudelka
Augusta Edwards Fine Art, Pace/MacGill
Gallery, Robert Koch Gallery

Anthony Koutras
Stephen Bulger Gallery

Kacper Kowalski
Atlas Gallery

Daniel Kramer
Fahey/Klein Gallery, Staley-Wise Gallery

Arnold Kramer
Joseph Bellows Gallery

Shai Kremer
Robert Koch Gallery

August Kreyenkamp
Contemporary Works/Vintage Works

Nico Krijno
Elizabeth Houston Gallery, Huxley-
Parlour Gallery

Vilem Kriz
Scott Nichols Gallery

Germaine Krull
Contemporary Works/Vintage Works,
GILLES PEYROULET & CIE, Jörg
Maaß Kunsthandel

Heinrich Kuhn
Contemporary Works/Vintage Works, Kicken
Berlin, Paul M. Hertzmann, Inc.

Mona Kuhn
Flowers Gallery, Galerie Catherine et André
Hug, Jackson Fine Art, Scott Nichols Gallery

Claudia Kunin
Contemporary Works/Vintage Works

Koichiro Kurita
Scott Nichols Gallery

Index

Annie Leibovitz
Fahey/Klein Gallery, GALERIE FRÉDÉRIC
GOT, Jörg Maaß Kunsthandel, Weinstein
Hammons Gallery

Neil Leifer
Fahey/Klein Gallery, Monroe Gallery
of Photography

Rita Leistner
Stephen Bulger Gallery

Saul Leiter
Galerie f5,6, Howard Greenberg Gallery, L.
Parker Stephenson Photographs

Lek & Sowat
Polka Galerie

Ysabel LeMay
Catherine Edelman Gallery

Fernando Lemos
Utópica

Elizabeth Lennard
GILLES PEYROULET & CIE

Gita Lenz
Gitterman Gallery

Herman Leonard
Catherine Edelman Gallery, Etherton Gallery,
Fahey/Klein Gallery, Robert Mann Gallery

Sze Tsung Nicolás Leong
Polka Galerie

Rebecca Lepkoff
Barry Singer Gallery

Helmar Lerski
Kicken Berlin

Henri Le Secq
Contemporary Works/Vintage Works, Hans
P. Kraus Jr. Inc., Robert Koch Gallery

Alfred Leslie
Bruce Silverstein Gallery

Adriana Lestido
Rolf Art

Laura Letinsky
Yancey Richardson Gallery

Randal Levenson
Joseph Bellows Gallery

Mikael Levin
GILLES PEYROULET & CIE

Joel D. Levinson
Contemporary Works/Vintage Works

Leon Levinstein
L. Parker Stephenson Photographs

Helen Levitt
Contemporary Works/Vintage Works,
Fraenkel Gallery, Galerie f5,6, LAURENCE
MILLER GALLERY, Richard Moore
Photographs, Robert Klein Gallery, Robert
Koch Gallery

Builder Levy
Arnika Dawkins Gallery Photographic
Fine Art

Andre Lichtenberg
Holden Luntz Gallery, Inc.

Roy Lichtenstein
BOCCARA ART

Katja Liebmann
HackelBury Fine Art

LIFE Picture
Archive Atlas Gallery

Michael Light
Atlas Gallery, Joseph Bellows Gallery

Index

M

Dora Maar
Contemporary Works/Vintage Works, GILLES PEYROULET & CIE, Robert Koch Gallery

Ian MacEachern
Stephen Bulger Gallery

John Mack
Robert Mann Gallery

Alex MacLean
Robert Koch Gallery, Yancey Richardson Gallery

Chema Madoz
PDNB Gallery

Xavier Magali
BOCCARA ART

René Magritte
Bruce Silverstein Gallery

Ute Mahler
Kicken Berlin

Werner Mahler
Kicken Berlin

Vivian Maier
Howard Greenberg Gallery, Huxley-Parlour Gallery

Thomas Mailaender
Michael Hoppen Gallery

David Maisel
Edwynn Houk Gallery

Alex Majoli
Howard Greenberg Gallery

Christopher Makos
Fahey/Klein Gallery

Rose Mandel
Deborah Bell Photographs, Richard Moore Photographs

Mike Mandel
Robert Mann Gallery

Gered Mankowitz
Atlas Gallery

Sally Mann
Edwynn Houk Gallery, Jackson Fine Art, Robert Koch Gallery

Esko Mannikko
Yancey Richardson Gallery

Constantine Manos
Robert Klein Gallery

Man Ray
Bruce Silverstein Gallery, Contemporary Works/Vintage Works, Edwynn Houk Gallery, Fahey/Klein Gallery, Hyperion Press, Ltd., Joel Soroka Gallery, Kicken Berlin, Paul M. Hertzmann, Inc., Robert Klein Gallery, Robert Koch Gallery

Werner Mantz
Kicken Berlin

Barbara Maples
PDNB Gallery

Robert Mapplethorpe
baudoin lebon gallery, Contemporary Works/Vintage Works, Weinstein Hammons Gallery, Yancey Richardson Gallery

Yves Marchand & Romain Meffre
Polka Galerie

Christian Marclay
Fraenkel Gallery

Index

Sanaz Mazinani
Stephen Bulger Gallery

Linda McCartney
James Hyman Gallery

Chirs McCaw
Candela Gallery

Steve McCurry
GALERIE FRÉDÉRIC GOT, Huxley-Parlour Gallery

Paul McDonough
Joseph Bellows Gallery

Ian McKeever
HackelBury Fine Art

Klea McKenna
Gitterman Gallery

Rhondal McKinney
PDNB Gallery

Meryl McMaster
Stephen Bulger Gallery

Joe McNally
Monroe Gallery of Photography

Ralph Eugene Meatyard
Contemporary Works/Vintage Works, Fraenkel Gallery

Francisco Medail
Rolf Art

Cheryl Medow
PDNB Gallery

Bernard C. Meeyers
Alan Klotz Gallery

Gianfranco Meggiato
BOCCARA ART

Susan Meiselas
Galerie Catherine et André Hug, Stephen Daiter Gallery

Roger Melis
Kicken Berlin

Philip Melnick
Joseph Bellows Gallery

Tony Mendoza
Lee Marks Fine Art

Vincent Mercier
Galerie Catherine et André Hug

Eugenio Merino
Unix Gallery

Annette Messager
Contemporary Works/Vintage Works

John Messinger
Atlas Gallery, Unix Gallery

Enrique Metinides
Toluca Fine Art

Ray K. Metzker
Catherine Couturier Gallery, Contemporary Works/Vintage Works, GALLERY 19/21, Howard Greenberg Gallery, LAURENCE MILLER GALLERY, only photography, Scheinbaum & Russek, Ltd.

Sheila Metzner
Contemporary Works/Vintage Works, Fahey/Klein Gallery, Staley-Wise Gallery

Baron Adolf De Meyer
Contemporary Works/Vintage Works

Joel Meyerowitz
The Halsted Gallery, Howard Greenberg Gallery, Huxley-Parlour Gallery, Polka Galerie

Duane Michals
Fahey/Klein Gallery

Index

Brad Moore
Fahey/Klein Gallery

Matthew Moore
Lisa Sette Gallery

Jean Moral
GILLES PEYROULET & CIE,
Gitterman Gallery

John Moran
William L. Schaeffer Photographic Works
of Art

Carlos Moreira
Utópica

Abelardo Morell
Edwynn Houk Gallery, Huxley-Parlour Gallery

Barbara Morgan
Bruce Silverstein Gallery, Contemporary
Works/Vintage Works, The Halsted Gallery,
Henry Feldstein, Scheinbaum & Russek, Ltd.,
Scott Nichols Gallery, Wach Gallery

Yasumasa Morimura
MEM, Inc.

Kazz Morishita
PDNB Gallery

Daido Moriyama
GALLERY 19/21, IBASHO

Wright Morris
Paul M. Hertzmann, Inc., Scott
Nichols Gallery

Mark Morrisroe
ClampArt

William Mortensen
Joseph Bellows Gallery

Ray Mortenson
L. Parker Stephenson Photographs

Keizo Motoda
MEM, Inc.

Felix Jacques Moulin
Contemporary Works/Vintage Works

Rodrigo Moya
Etherton Gallery

Grant Mudford
Joseph Bellows Gallery

Zanele Muholi
Yancey Richardson Gallery

Michael Mulno
Joseph Bellows Gallery

Vik Muniz
Contemporary Works/Vintage Works,
Edwynn Houk Gallery

Nickolas Muray
Fahey/Klein Gallery, PDNB Gallery,
Throckmorton Fine Art, Inc.

Dr. John Murray
Contemporary Works/Vintage Works

Fakir Musafar
Fahey/Klein Gallery

Eadweard Muybridge
Etherton Gallery, Henry Feldstein, Joseph
Bellows Gallery, Paul M. Hertzmann, Inc.,
Richard Moore Photographs, Robert Koch
Gallery, Scheinbaum & Russek, Ltd., Scott
Nichols Gallery

Carl Mydans
Contemporary Works/Vintage Works,
Monroe Gallery of Photography

Index

Nadezda Nikolova-Kratzer
HackelBury Fine Art

Magnus Nilsson
Weinstein Hammons Gallery

Wang Ningde
Bryce Wolkowitz Gallery

Sohei Nishino
Bryce Wolkowitz Gallery, Michael
Hoppen Gallery

Lori Nix
Catherine Edelman Gallery, ClampArt

Nicholas Nixon
Fraenkel Gallery

Claude Nori
Polka Galerie

Dorothy Norman
Contemporary Works/Vintage Works

C. Michael Norton
Unix Gallery

Marina Núñez
RocioSantaCruz

O

Ian Patrick O'Connor
Momentum Fine Art

P.H. Oelman
Henry Feldstein

Naoyuki Ogino
IBASHO

Kumi Oguro
IBASHO

Mitsugu Ohnishi
PGI

Kaoru Ohto
Kicken Berlin

J.D. 'Okhai Ojeikere
L. Parker Stephenson Photographs

Kosuke Okahara
only photography, Polka Galerie

Toby Old
Fahey/Klein Gallery

Jules Olitski
BOCCARA ART

Francis Olschfskie
Alan Klotz Gallery

Katsumi Omori
MEM, Inc.

Terry O'Neill
La Galerie de l'Instant

Shigeru Onishi
GALLERY 19/21, MEM, Inc.

Ruth Orkin
Catherine Couturier Gallery, The
Halsted Gallery, PDNB Gallery, Stephen
Bulger Gallery

Marinus J. Ortelee
Contemporary Works/Vintage Works

Pablo Ortiz
Monasterio Toluca Fine Art

Christine Osinski
Joseph Bellows Gallery

Index

Martin Parr
Huxley-Parlour Gallery, Stephen
Daiter Gallery

Rondal Partridge
Scott Nichols Gallery

Malcolm Pasley
Robert Koch Gallery

Esteban Pastorino Diaz
PDNB Gallery

Lois Patino
RocioSantaCruz

Wendy Paton
Sous Les Etoiles Gallery

Brendan Pattengale
Fahey/Klein Gallery

Jonathan Paul
Unix Gallery

Frank Paulin
Bruce Silverstein Gallery, Contemporary
Works/Vintage Works

Susan Paulsen
Deborah Bell Photographs

Vesna Pavlovi
Laufer

Paolo Pellegrin
La Galerie de l'Instant

Irving Penn
Alan Klotz Gallery, Atlas Gallery,
Contemporary Works/Vintage Works, Fahey/
Klein Gallery, Gitterman Gallery, The Halsted
Gallery, Michael Shapiro Photographs, Pace/
MacGill Gallery, Robert Koch Gallery, Scott
Nichols Gallery

Gilles Peress
L. Parker Stephenson Photographs

Marta María Pérez Bravo
PDNB Gallery

Francesco Pergolesi
Catherine Edelman Gallery

Jean-Marie Périer
Fahey/Klein Gallery, Polka Galerie

Rachel Perry
Yancey Richardson Gallery

Gösta Peterson
Deborah Bell Photographs

Charles Petillon
Sous Les Etoiles Gallery

John Pfahl
Joseph Bellows Gallery

Stephanie Pfriender Stylander
La Galerie de l'Instant

Simone Pheulpin
BOCCARA ART

Rachel Phillips
Catherine Couturier Gallery

Denis Piel
Staley-Wise Gallery

Pierre-Louis Pierson
Contemporary Works/Vintage Works

Jack Pierson
ClampArt

Ave Pildas
Richard Moore Photographs

Matthew Pillsbury
Edwynn Houk Gallery, Jackson Fine Art

Sándor Pinczehelyi
Robert Koch Gallery

Index

Q

R

Arnulf Rainer
Paul M. Hertzmann, Inc.

Daniel Ranalli
LAURENCE MILLER GALLERY

Rankin
Fahey/Klein Gallery

Edward Ranney
Deborah Bell Photographs

Alan Rath
Bryce Wolkowitz Gallery

Priscilla Rattazzi
Staley-Wise Gallery

Bill Ray
Monroe Gallery of Photography

Tony Ray-Jones
Alan Klotz Gallery, James Hyman Gallery

Paul Reas
James Hyman Gallery

Verner Reed
Monroe Gallery of Photography

Vilém Reichmann
GALLERY 19/21, Robert Koch Gallery

Dusan Reljin
Laufer

René-Jacques
Hyperion Press, Ltd.

Albert Renger-Patzsch
Contemporary Works/Vintage Works, Kicken
Berlin, Robert Koch Gallery

Andreas Rentsch
Candela Gallery

Marcia Resnick
Deborah Bell Photographs, Paul M.
Hertzmann, Inc.

Nancy Rexroth
Weinstein Hammons Gallery

Antonio Reynoso
Charles Isaacs Photography, Inc.

Marc Riboud
Atlas Gallery, L. Parker Stephenson
Photographs, Polka Galerie, Scott
Nichols Gallery

Eugene Richards
Fahey/Klein Gallery, Stephen Daiter Gallery

Bob Richardson
Staley-Wise Gallery

Nancy Richardson
Voltz Clarke Gallery

Evelyn Richter
Kicken Berlin

Gerhard Richter
Jörg Maaß Kunsthandel

Heinrich Riebesehl
Kicken Berlin

Meghann Riepenhoff
Jackson Fine Art

Javier Riera
Sous Les Etoiles Gallery

Ringl + Pit
Deborah Bell Photographs

Klaus Rinke
Kicken Berlin

Index

Aristotle Roufanis
Momentum Fine Art

Georges Rousse
Sous Les Etoiles Gallery

Paolo Roversi
Pace/MacGill Gallery

Michal Rovner
Pace/MacGill Gallery

Josh Rowell
Unix Gallery

Kourtney Roy
Galerie Catherine et André Hug

Ian Ruhter
Fahey/Klein Gallery

Tokyo Rumando
IBASHO

Ed Ruscha
Yancey Richardson Gallery

Grant Rusk
Joseph Bellows Gallery

John Ruskin
Hans P. Kraus Jr. Inc.

Rae Russel
Barry Singer Gallery

Andrew Joseph Russell
Contemporary Works/Vintage Works, Lee
Gallery, William L. Schaeffer Photographic
Works of Art

Felipe Russo
Utópica

Drahomír Josef Ruzicka
Robert Koch Gallery

Ryuijie
GALLERY 19/21

Graciela Sacco
Rolf Art

Chiyuki Sakagami
MEM, Inc.

Heihachiro Sakai
MEM, Inc.

Armando Salas Portugal
Charles Isaacs Photography, Inc.

Sebastião Salgado
Fahey/Klein Gallery, Huxley-Parlour Gallery,
Peter Fetterman Gallery, Polka Galerie,
Robert Klein Gallery, Scheinbaum &
Russek, Ltd., Scott Nichols Gallery, Yancey
Richardson Gallery

Keris Salmon
Arnika Dawkins Gallery Photographic Fine Art

Auguste Salzmann
Alan Klotz Gallery, Charles Isaacs
Photography, Inc., Contemporary Works/
Vintage Works, Gary Edwards Gallery

Connie Samaras
De Soto Gallery

Victoria Sambunaris
Yancey Richardson Gallery

Pentti Sammallahti
Etherton Gallery

Lourdes Sanchez
Sears-Peyton Gallery

August Sander
Deborah Bell Photographs, The Halsted
Gallery, Joseph Bellows Gallery, Kicken
Berlin, Paul M. Hertzmann, Inc., Robert Koch
Gallery, Yancey Richardson Gallery

Index

Zack Seckler
ClampArt

Volker Seding
Stephen Bulger Gallery

Norman Seeff
Fahey/Klein Gallery

George Seeley
Contemporary Works/Vintage Works

Tomio Seike
Galerie f5,6, PGI

Alfred Seiland
Kicken Berlin

Peter Sekaer
Richard Moore Photographs

Shosuke Sekioka
MEM, Inc.

Mark Seliger
Fahey/Klein Gallery

Andres Serrano
Scheinbaum & Russek, Ltd.

Jose Maria Sert
Charles Isaacs Photography, Inc.

Rick Shaefer
Sears-Peyton Gallery

Ben Shahn
Richard Moore Photographs

Manjari Sharma
ClampArt

Mark Shaw
Monroe Gallery of Photography

Art Shay
Monroe Gallery of Photography

Fazal Sheikh
Pace/MacGill Gallery

Toshio Shibata
IBASHO, LAURENCE MILLER GALLERY,
only photography, Polka Galerie

William Gordon Shields
Joseph Bellows Gallery

Osamu Shiihara
Contemporary Works/Vintage Works, L.
Parker Stephenson Photographs, MEM, Inc.

KwangHo Shin
Unix Gallery

Benjamin Shine
BOCCARA ART

SATO Shintaro
PGI

Melissa Shook
Joseph Bellows Gallery

Stephen Shore
Edwynn Houk Gallery

Julius Shulman
Alan Klotz Gallery, Contemporary Works/
Vintage Works, Fahey/Klein Gallery

Malick Sidibé
HackelBury Fine Art, L. Parker
Stephenson Photographs

Jeanloup Sieff
Atlas Gallery

Arthur Siegel
Contemporary Works/Vintage Works

Ed Sievers
Robert Mann Gallery

William Silano
Deborah Bell Photographs

Index

Rosalind Fox Solomon
Bruce Silverstein Gallery, Stephen
Bulger Gallery

Stephen Somerstein
Fahey/Klein Gallery

Frederick Sommer
Bruce Silverstein Gallery, Etherton Gallery,
Michael Shapiro Photographs, Paul M.
Hertzmann, Inc., Richard Moore Photographs

Jacques Sonck
L. Parker Stephenson Photographs

Trine Søndergaard
Bruce Silverstein Gallery

Wayne Sorce
Joseph Bellows Gallery

Alec Soth
Fraenkel Gallery, Huxley-Parlour Gallery,
Jörg Maaß Kunsthandel, Weinstein
Hammons Gallery

Montserrat Soto
RocioSantaCruz

Brea Souders
Bruce Silverstein Gallery

Jem Southam
Robert Mann Gallery

Southworth & Hawes
Contemporary Works/Vintage Works

Jerry Spagnoli
Contemporary Works/Vintage Works

Vee Speers
Fahey/Klein Gallery, Jackson Fine Art

Suzy Spence
Sears-Peyton Gallery

Fritz Spiess
Stephen Bulger Gallery

Guillermo Srodek-Hart
Utópica

Peter Stackpole
Paul M. Hertzmann, Inc., Scott Nichols Gallery

Anton Stankowski
Kicken Berlin

Doug and Mike Starn
HackelBury Fine Art, Lisa Sette Gallery

Edward Steichen
Charles Isaacs Photography, Inc.,
Contemporary Works/Vintage Works,
Gitterman Gallery, Keith de Lellis Gallery, Lee
Gallery, Paul M. Hertzmann, Inc., Staley-
Wise Gallery, Wach Gallery

Amy Stein
ClampArt, Robert Koch Gallery

Andre Steiner
Gitterman Gallery

Ralph Steiner
The Halsted Gallery, Scheinbaum & Russek,
Ltd., Scott Nichols Gallery

Otto Steinert
Jörg Maaß Kunsthandel, Kicken Berlin, L.
Parker Stephenson Photographs

Richard Steinheimer
Robert Mann Gallery

Mark Steinmetz
Jackson Fine Art, Yancey Richardson Gallery

Prue Stent & Honey Long
Fahey/Klein Gallery

Joseph Sterling
only photography, Stephen Daiter Gallery

Index

Kazuo Sumida
LAURENCE MILLER GALLERY

Maria Svarbova
Momentum Fine Art

Julianne Swartz
Lisa Sette Gallery

Charles Swedlund
Stephen Daiter Gallery

Homer Sykes
James Hyman Gallery

Joseph Szabo
Gitterman Gallery

François Szalay Colos
Richard Moore Photographs

Kálmán Szijártó
Robert Koch Gallery

Gabor Szilasi
Stephen Bulger Gallery

T

Maurice Tabard
GALLERY 19/21, Gitterman Gallery,
Hyperion Press, Ltd.

Isaiah W. Taber
Scott Nichols Gallery, William L. Schaeffer
Photographic Works of Art

Munemasa Takahashi
PGI

Yutaka Takanashi
only photography

Motohiro Takeda
IBASHO

Hiroyuki Takenouchi
PGI

William Henry Fox Talbot
Charles Isaacs Photography, Inc., Gary
Edwards Gallery, Hans P. Kraus Jr. Inc.,
Robert Koch Gallery

Dominique Tarlé
La Galerie de l'Instant

Dain Tasker
Joseph Bellows Gallery, Paul M.
Hertzmann, Inc.

George Tatge
Galerie Catherine et André Hug

Paulette Tavormina
Robert Klein Gallery, Robert Mann Gallery

Maggie Taylor
Candela Gallery, Catherine Couturier Gallery

Jack D. Teemer
Joseph Bellows Gallery

Marjan Teeuwen
Bruce Silverstein Gallery

Esther Teichmann
Flowers Gallery

Evandro Teixeira
Utópica

Rubens Teixeira Scavone
RocioSantaCruz

Val Telberg
LAURENCE MILLER GALLERY

Index

U

Raoul Ubac
GILLES PEYROULET & CIE

Diego Uchitel
Fahey/Klein Gallery

Shoji Ueda
L. Parker Stephenson Photographs

Jerry Uelsmann
Contemporary Works/Vintage Works, The
Halsted Gallery, Scheinbaum & Russek, Ltd.

Lloyd Ullberg
Barry Singer Gallery

Doris Ulmann
Contemporary Works/Vintage Works, Keith
de Lellis Gallery

Brian Ulrich
Robert Koch Gallery

Umbo (Otto Umbehr)
Kicken Berlin, L. Parker
Stephenson Photographs

Penelope Umbrico
Bruce Silverstein Gallery

Barry Underwood
Sous Les Etoiles Gallery

Martin Usborne
Lee Marks Fine Art

Tokuko Ushioda
PGI

V

Tony Vaccaro
Monroe Gallery of Photography

Roger Vail
Joseph Bellows Gallery

Gabriel Valansi
Rolf Art

Manolo Valdes
BOCCARA ART

Mauricio Valenzuela
Augusta Edwards Fine Art

Rodrigo Valenzuela
LAURENCE MILLER GALLERY

Al Vandenberg
Augusta Edwards Fine Art

Ed van der Elsken
Galerie f5,6, Kicken Berlin

Ron van Dongen
Catherine Edelman Gallery

Geza Vandor
Contemporary Works/Vintage Works, Robert
Koch Gallery

Willard Van Dyke
Michael Shapiro Photographs, Paul
M. Hertzmann, Inc., Richard Moore
Photographs, Scheinbaum & Russek, Ltd.

Jindrich Vanek
Joel Soroka Gallery

Ruud Van Empel
Huxley-Parlour Gallery, Jackson Fine Art

Jörn Vanhöfen
Robert Mann Gallery

Index

W

Todd Walker
Etherton Gallery

Edward Wallowitch
Deborah Bell Photographs

Andy Warhol
BOCCARA ART

Julian Wasser
Fahey/Klein Gallery

Carleton E. Watkins
Charles Isaacs Photography, Inc.,
The Halsted Gallery, Lee Gallery, Paul
M. Hertzmann, Inc., Richard Moore
Photographs, Robert Koch Gallery, Scott
Nichols Gallery, William L. Schaeffer
Photographic Works of Art

Margaret Watkins
Robert Mann Gallery

Albert Watson
Contemporary Works/Vintage Works, Holden
Luntz Gallery, Inc.

Alex Webb
Etherton Gallery, Robert Klein Gallery,
Robert Koch Gallery, Stephen Bulger Gallery,
Stephen Daiter Gallery

Todd Webb
Richard Moore Photographs, Scheinbaum
& Russek, Ltd., Scott Nichols Gallery, Todd
Webb Archive, Yancey Richardson Gallery

Rebecca Norris Webb
Robert Koch Gallery

Bruce Weber
Fahey/Klein Gallery, La Galerie de l'Instant

Charles Weed
Paul M. Hertzmann, Inc.

Weegee
Barry Singer Gallery, Catherine Couturier
Gallery, Elizabeth Houston Gallery, Henry
Feldstein, Keith de Lellis Gallery, Richard
Moore Photographs, Robert Mann Gallery,
William L. Schaeffer Photographic Works of
Art, Winter Works on Paper

Eric Weeks
Galerie Catherine et André Hug

Carrie Mae Weems
Scheinbaum & Russek, Ltd.

William Wegman
Huxley-Parlour Gallery, Lisa Sette Gallery

Shen Wei
Flowers Gallery

Harley Weir
Michael Hoppen Gallery

Sabine Weiss
Contemporary Works/Vintage Works,
Stephen Daiter Gallery

Susann Wellm
Sous Les Etoiles Gallery

Jack Welpott
Contemporary Works/Vintage Works, Joseph
Bellows Gallery, Scott Nichols Gallery

Qin Wen
Hyperion Press, Ltd.

Donata Wenders
Polka Galerie

Fu Wenjun
BOCCARA ART

Alfred Wertheimer
Fahey/Klein Gallery, Staley-Wise Gallery

Henry Wessel
Robert Mann Gallery

Index

Jeffrey Wolin
Catherine Edelman Gallery

John Wood
Bruce Silverstein Gallery

Myron Wood
Scheinbaum & Russek, Ltd.

Tom Wood
Augusta Edwards Fine Art

C.D. Woodley
Stephen Bulger Gallery

Francesca Woodman
Gary Edwards Gallery, Robert Klein Gallery

Willard E. Worden
Scott Nichols Gallery

Witho Worms
L. Parker Stephenson Photographs

Susan Worsham
Candela Gallery

Don Worth
The Halsted Gallery, Scott Nichols Gallery

Magdalena Wosinska
Fahey/Klein Gallery

Bastiaan Woudt
ackson Fine Art

Willie Anne Wright
Candela Gallery

Bruce Wrighton
LAURENCE MILLER GALLERY,
only photography

Ida Wyman
Catherine Couturier Gallery, Monroe Gallery
of Photography

Llewellyn Xavier
Unix Gallery

Kiyoshi Yagi
PGI

José Yalenti
Utópica

Noriko Yamaguchi
MEM, Inc.

Masao Yamamoto
Etherton Gallery, Jackson Fine Art, Robert
Koch Gallery, Yancey Richardson Gallery

Mariana Yampolsky
Throckmorton Fine Art, Inc.

Frank Yamrus
ClampArt

Shin Yanagisawa
only photography

Marc Yankus
ClampArt

Nicolas Yantchevsky
La Galerie de l'Instant

David Yarrow
Holden Luntz Gallery, Inc.

Index